Maria Chiara Martinelli

How to Eat Out in Italy

How to understand the menu and make yourself understood

Dictionary and Phrase Book for the Restaurant

GREMESE

English translation:
Michelle Dunne

Jacket design:
Carlo Soldatini

Drawings:
Maria Rosaria Paradisi

Phototypeset by:
Prom.edi. srl - Rome

Printed and bound by:
SO.GRA.TE. - Città di Castello (PG)

© 1997 Gremese International
P.O. Box 14335
00149 Rome - Italy

ISBN 88-7301-095-4

Italy is not only world famous for its art treasures and its natural beauty, but also for its cooking.

To visit Italy and only see its monuments would mean missing out on its rich gastronomic tradition, given that cooking is such an important part of any people's culture. And above all, it would be a shame to travel to Italy and not to get to know better, what is recognized as one of the best cuisines in the world!

In Italy, eating is not just regarded as a physical need but as a discovery, a journey through the history, culture and creativity of a nation which has resulted in the transformation of a few simple ingredients into tasty dishes which are now famous throughout the world.

We believe that foreign visitors to Italy should not just approach this country's cuisine in a casual way but they should arm themselves with a basic knowledge so that they can make the best choices. In this way they do not risk missing out on the chance of tasting some of the best things in the right places.

This guide aims to offer foreign tourists a complete picture of Italian cooking: its characteristics, its products and most typical dishes and the best places to try them, the right words and phrases to understand and make yourself understood in a restaurant. The guide offers a selection of the "most Italian" recipes and those which are easiest to make when you return to your own country (especially if you have the chance to take home some genuine products such as olive oil and Parmesan cheese) so that you can remember and relive some of the more enjoyable moments of your holiday in Italy.

MAIN CHARACTERISTICS OF ITALIAN COOKING

Italian cooking, which is based mainly on typical products of the Mediterranean regions, can be described as a poor man's cuisine that has been enriched by the traditions of the rich courtiers who governed the various regions in Italy centuries ago. The convents and monasteries also made their mark in gastronomic terms with their works of art in cakes and pastries. In general terms, Italy can be divided into two distinctive parts from a gastronomic point of view: the North, where the cuisine is characterized by more delicate flavors and where butter is used as the basic ingredient, and the Center-South where oil is the main ingredient for seasoning and the dishes have a strong, often spicy flavor.

In recent years however, this division has become less noticeable with new non-traditional dishes coming from various regions, which aspire more or less directly to *nouvelle cuisine*. Vegetables and aromatic herbs have always been used throughout Italy, while spices are not used much with the exception of pepper and, in the South, chili pepper.

In addition to vegetables and herbs, pasta is obviously one of the basics of Italian cuisine with its many shapes. With or without filling, pasta changes flavor all the time depending on its size. It is unlikely that you will have tried real pasta at its best in another country unless you have had it in a "true" Italian restaurant. Try having some pasta, reminding the waiter to bring it *al dente* (not over-cooked, chewy) and you'll notice the difference. And don't just go for the more common seasonings such as tomato sauce and *ragù* (meat sauce), but discover the many ways in which pasta can be flavored, resulting in lots of varied dishes.

Fish and seafood also have an important place in Italian cuisine: given that some restaurants use frozen fish, especially in the winter, it is advisable to ask so as to be sure that the fish is fresh. Generally the best fish is found in coastal areas but also in the big cities such as Rome, Milan and Turin.

The meat in some regions such as Tuscany is excellent, whereas perhaps in other regions, such as some areas in the South, fresh fish is of a better standard. Naturally, it must be noted that the quality of the food is not just linked to the area but also to the quality of the restaurant.

Other products for which Italy is famous include cheese, cold cut meats, bread, and wine. Every region, if not every district, has its own typical products resulting in an infinite variety of these foods. Even if the better known products are available throughout Italy, it is worth checking out the local specialties as it is unlikely that you will find the very same product in other areas.

Then there are many confectionary specialties which are often traditionally linked to the various religious feasts. These are available in restaurants and especially in the many confectionary shops.

THE ITALIAN MENU

The classic Italian menu has four courses plus dessert.
It usually starts with an hors-d'œuvre which typically consists of a selection of cold cut meats, olives and pickles. There is, however, an endless variety of cold or hot starters to choose from. They are generally just tasters rather than regular portions. The first course, which is either pasta, rice or soup, follows. There is a great temptation to indulge in the offerings of the Italian culinary imagination, so the choice is always ample. In many restaurants you can ask for a reduced portion of three types of pasta instead of choosing just one. The second course is either fish or meat and again the choice in most restaurants is quite varied. Cooked vegetables or a salad can also be ordered on the side.
You can ask for a mixed cheeseboard before dessert and then finish the meal with fruit (whole or salad) or with ice-cream or cake.
The typical Italian custom of having an espresso coffee after a meal can be very enjoyable. It is much more concentrated and aromatic than the coffee drunk in other countries and is often followed by a liqueur or an *amaro* (bitter liqueur) chosen from the best of the national repertoire or local liqueurs as recommended by the waiter.

RESTAURANTS IN ITALY

There is an enormous variety of places to go and eat out in Italy offering a wide choice, also in terms of prices.
Most hotels have their own restaurant and the quality varies from one hotel to the next but they are generally quite good.

The best way to get to know Italian cooking is to go to a real *ristorante* (restaurant) where you will find typical local dishes - in a word, more "real."

There are many elegant restaurants in the big cities and in the tourist and holiday resorts which offer a refined menu inspired by *nouvelle cuisine*, by variations of traditional dishes or reduced according to the dictates of modern cooking. The wine list in these places usually offers a wide selection of some of the best national and foreign wines. The atmosphere is usually very relaxed, with luxury furnishings; such places usually have only a few tables and it is advisable to make a reservation. Naturally, the prices are in line with the elegance and menu of the restaurant.

However, the majority of restaurants are reasonably priced, have a pleasant atmosphere and a varied menu.

If you want to experience real Italian cooking, you should avoid the restaurants with "special tourist menus" as the price is the only advantage. Many of the restaurants which are particularly popular among tourists do not offer a very interesting range of dishes, in order to cater for the mixed clientele, which in reality have nothing to do with real Italian cooking.

It is a good idea to stick to the restaurants or *trattorias* (the name indicates the type of place which offers tasty, traditional country cooking and does not claim to be elegant, just genuine) which can be found off the beaten track, hidden in the side streets of the city far from the main streets, or in the little country roads. It is in these places, where you are more likely to find the locals than tourists, that you will experience real Italian cooking and at very reasonable prices.

The menu is often limited to just a few dishes which are based on the gastronomic tradition of the area, on local products and their availability depending on the season. Even if the wine list does not offer a wide choice, it will include the best and most genuine wines of the area.

It is not always essential to book a table (depending on the number of tables available and how busy the restaurant is), but it is better to do so in order to be sure, especially on Saturday evenings and Sunday lunch time.

It is well worth trying the local pizzeria, at least once, which is very popular with young people. Pizza, the main course of the meal, varies greatly from the classic *Margherita* to the more imaginative, richer pizzas. It is, in any case, a very inexpensive meal. In most of these places you can order lots of other types of dishes in addition or as an alternative to pizza.

Specialized restaurants, a recent phenomenon over the last few years, have become increasingly popular: for example, there are restaurants where you can order pasta only, lots of different types obviously, or places where you can go just to enjoy an absolutely perfect steak cooked Florentine style.

In any case, it is a good idea to read the menu and price list, which are usually displayed at the entrance of the restaurant, before choosing where to go and eat. By doing so you get an idea of the choice available on the menu and the prices.

Major credit cards are accepted in most restaurants, especially in the big cities and those which are particularly popular among tourists. Some small and medium-sized restaurants, especially in the central and southern regions do not accept credit cards. Naturally, prices vary according to the type of restaurant. The average prices of a full meal, including drinks, is around Lit. 30 - 40,000 per person. Prices are higher for fresh fish. You often spend less in the *trattorias* and are still full at the end of the meal.

The bill in restaurants, trattorias or pizzerias includes taxes, the cover charge and service. However, most people leave a tip for the waiter of a few thousand lire in proportion to the bill.

One last word with regard to the opening hours : restaurants and trattorias are open for lunch from around midday to 2.30 P.M. and from 7 P.M. to 10.30 P.M. in the evening. These hours vary depending on the region (in the central and southern regions, people generally eat later and the opening hours are slightly later) and on the season (the restaurants, especially in the holiday resorts stay open longer during the summer). Pizzerias usually open only in the evening, although there are exceptions.

Cheese production in Italy is vast and diversified. In fact Italy is one of the countries with the greatest number of typical cheeses, some of which are famous abroad. In many cases these are original products, protected by consortiums which guarantee their quality and defend them against imitations. The following is a brief description of the more common cheeses indicating the region they come from. Naturally the list is not at all complete given that there are hundreds of different types of cheese produced throughout the country. As for all products, it is a good idea to ask the waiter's advice when you wish to taste the more typical cheeses in a certain area.

Asiago: Veneto. Half fat, made with cow's milk, of medium consistency, it is pale yellow in color and the cheese is full of small holes. A fresh version is available which has a sweeter flavor, while the mature version is harder and slightly spicy.

Burrata: Apulia/ Campania. This fresh cheese, made with cow's milk, is smooth and white on the outside, and the inside contains butter or a type of minced mozzarella mixed with cream. The flavor is sweet and subtle and very fresh.

Caciocavallo: Southern regions. This is a hard, smooth cheese made with cow's milk and is pale yellow in color; the fresh cheese has a sweet flavor while the mature cheese is slightly spicy. A smoked version of this cheese also exists.

Caciotta: Central regions. This cheese is quite small, flat and round in shape. It can be made with cow's or goat's milk or a mixture of the two. It is a soft cheese, yellow in color and is eaten fresh; the flavor can be subtle or slightly spicy.

Canestrato: Apulia/Sardinia. This is a hard, mature cheese which is generally made with goat's milk and has quite a spicy flavor.

Castelmagno: Piemonte. This is a semi-hard cheese, ivory white in color which darkens as it matures. The flavor of the mature cheese is delicate at first and then it becomes strong and spicy.

Fiore sardo: Sardinia. This cheese which is made with goat's milk is compact and varies in color from white to pale yellow. The spiciness of the cheese depends on its degree of maturity. It is very commonly served on a cheeseboard or grated.

Fontina: Valle d'Aosta. This cheese is made with cow's milk, is elastic in texture, yellow in color with small holes, and a strong but not spicy flavor. It is mainly used for the *Fonduta* (see section on "National Dishes").

Gorgonzola: Lombardy. This cheese is white in color with green threads running through it and is soft in texture. It is made with cow's milk and has a strong flavor and smell.

Grana padano: North-western regions. Hard cheese, made with cow's milk , mature and flavored. It is generally grated on pasta dishes but is also excellent at the end of a meal, especially with pears.

Mascarpone: Lombardy. This is a creamy, sweet, fat product which is mainly used for making exquisite pastries or for seasoning pasta dishes.

Mozzarella di bufala: Campania. This is a fresh cheese, which is soft and elastic, white in color and produced in small round shapes. The flavor is delicate and fresh and slightly bitter. The buffalo mozzarella cheese made with buffalo's milk is softer and tastier than that made with cow's milk.

Parmigiano Reggiano: Emilia-Romagna. This is the most

CHEESES

famous of the Italian cheeses. It is similar to the cheese from the Po region but it is more highly esteemed, hard and rough, flavored, very commonly used in the grated form but it is also excellent as a starter or at the end of a meal.

Pecorino: Latium / Sardinia / Tuscany / Sicily. Made with goat's milk, this cheese is white in color when fresh and pale yellow when mature. Its characteristics vary slightly depending on the region, but it is a hard, strong-flavored cheese which is quite spicy.

Provolone: Southern regions/ Lombardy. This cheese is semi-hard, smooth and clear in color. Two versions exist, one of which is sweet and delicately flavored while the other is spicy.

Ricotta: All regions. This is a fresh, creamy, low-fat product which is made with cow's or goat's milk. It is mainly used for making desserts or as a filling for fresh pasta. In the southern regions, a mature version also exists which is called "hard ricotta" or "salty ricotta." It is quite spicy and is only used as a grated cheese.

Robiola: Piemonte / Lombardy. Fresh, creamy white cheese ideal for spreading on bread.

Stracchino: Lombardy. Soft fresh, white cheese with a delicate flavor. It is also known as *crescenza* meaning growth.

Taleggio: Lombardy. Full, fat cheese made with cow's milk, soft and buttery with a slightly bitter flavor and clear in color.

There is not a single region in Italy which cannot boast of a rich tradition of working with pork and obviously a whole range of products have been created as a result. In some areas, in addition to pork cold cuts, they make high quality products from other types of meat such as wild boar hams for example.

Some of these products are very famous outside Italy but many of the less well-known products are certainly worth trying.

Bresaola: Lombardy. This is a cold cut made with very lean bovine meat and is large in shape and uniform in color, dark red. It can be matured and is usually eaten as an hors-d'œuvre, thinly sliced and seasoned with oil, lemon and pepper.

Cacciatorini: Small cold cuts, the meat of which is minced coarsely, seasoned, flavored but not spicy. It is found throughout Italy.

Capocollo: Central and southern regions. This is the name given to this dark red cold cut in the central and southern regions. It is streaked with fat and is known as *coppa* in the northern regions.

Coppa (1): Emilia-Romagna. A matured cold cut which is mostly lean but streaked with fat; it is a well-known product in the Piacenza area. It is generally eaten as a starter together with other cold cut meats or as a country snack eaten with bread.

Coppa (2): Central regions. This cold cut is very different from its namesake in Emilia-Romagna: it is made from the less desirable parts of the pig (the head, snout etc.), cooked with herbs and vegetables, left to cool and pressed. It is usually eaten in a salad with olives, celery etc., resulting in a very tasty starter.

Cotechino: Made into sausages to be eaten cooked from a seasoned pork's meat-base mixture, lard and rind. This is made almost exclusively in the winter and is typical of the mixed boiled dishes in the North during this period.

Culatello: Parma. High quality specialty made from an extract of the pig's hind leg; it is lean, mature but soft, sweet and full flavored.

Finocchiona: Tuscany. Cold cut meat, soft in texture, flavored with fennel seeds and garlic.

Fiocchetto: This is also a specialty from Tuscany which is made from the pig's hind leg together with the renowned *Culatello*. This is a lean meat with streaks of fat and is apparently similar to *coppa (1)* but is sweeter and less spicy.

Mortadella: Produced in all regions but it is characteristic of Bologna in particular. It is a cold cut meat which is large in diameter, pinkish in color with flecks of lard. This meat has a distinctive taste and is flavored with black pepper and sometimes with pistachio nuts.

Prosciutto: This is one of the most famous products of Italian cuisine. It is made from an extract of the pig's hind leg which is then salted, matured and eaten raw. It can be soft and sweet or dry and flavorsome and is one of the best starters if combined with fruit such as melon or figs. The best known products are San Daniele from the Friuli region and Parma, both of which are soft in texture and sweet.

Salame: This is a sausage containing quite a fine textured mixture but contains quite a high fat content. Various types exist and those worth a mention include salami from Felino (Emilia-Romagna), the salami from Varzi, flavored with garlic, the salami from Ferrara (Emilia-Romagna) strongly flavored with garlic *salame d'la duja* (Piemonte), which is kept in containers full of lard, the *Milano* salami, made from a fine and fairly homogenous mixture, the *Secondigliano* from the Campania region, which is made spicy by the red hot chili peppers in the mixture.

Soppressa: Veneto. This is a type of salami made with a coarse mixture.

Soppressata: Central and southern regions. It is similar to a salami but it is oval as opposed to round; a particularly well-known product is Fabriano (Marche region), which is easy to identify as the pieces of lard are square.

Speck: Trentino-Alto Adige. Smoked raw ham, very lean and surrounded by a layer of fat.

Zampone: Emilia-Romagna. This cold cut meat is eaten cooked and is full-flavored, similar to *cotechino*. It is traditionally eaten on New Year's Eve with lentils.

PASTA

There is an infinite variety of pasta shapes in Italy which can be divided into several categories: dry pasta, egg pasta, egg filled, and homemade with water and flour. The following is a list of the more common shapes so you can identify them as pasta when you see them on the menu.

Dry pasta: Bavette, bigoli, bombolotti, bucatini, cannolicchi, capellini, conchiglie, conchiglioni, ditali, eliche, farfalle, fusilli, gnocchetti, maccheroncini, maccheroni, penne, pennette, pici, rigatoni, spaghetti, tonnarelli, tortiglioni, vermicelli, zite.

Egg pasta: Fettuccine, lagane, lasagne, maccheroni (or spaghetti) alla chitarra, pappardelle, tagliatelle, tagliolini.

Egg filled pasta: Agnolini, agnolotti, anolini, cannelloni, cappelletti, pansotti, ravioli, tortelli, tortellini.

Homemade pasta with water and flour: Cavatelli (or cavatieddi), maccheroni al ferro, orecchiette.

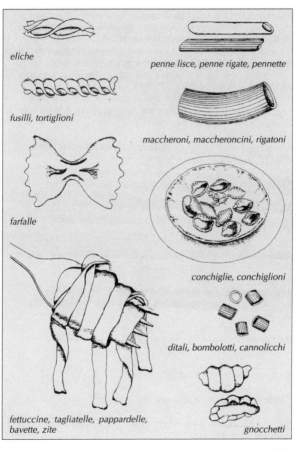

eliche

penne lisce, penne rigate, pennette

fusilli, tortiglioni

maccheroni, maccheroncini, rigatoni

farfalle

conchiglie, conchiglioni

ditali, bombolotti, cannolicchi

fettuccine, tagliatelle, pappardelle,
bavette, zite

gnocchetti

Italy is one of the most famous wine producing countries in the world. Hundreds of different types of wines are produced including whites, reds, rosé and liqueurs.
An entire volume would be needed to name or describe all of them, so we will restrict ourselves to a brief reference to the best and better known wines, indicating the region or area which they come from.

Aglianico del Vulture: Basilicata. Red, dry, suitable for red meats.

Albana: Emilia-Romagna. White, dry and pleasant with an alcohol content of around 12%.

Alcamo: Sicily. White, dry and fruity.

Aleatico: Apulia. Red, sweet, full-bodied with an alcohol content of around 15%; there is also a liqueur version which is about 18% proof.

Amarone: Veneto. Full-bodied red, strong flavor and is very suitable for roasts and red meats.

Asti spumante: Piemonte. This is one of the best known Italian sparkling wines, sweet, aromatic, very suitable for desserts.

Barbaresco: Piemonte. Red, dry, full-bodied, slightly aged; around 12% proof.

Barbera: Piemonte. Red, dry, rich.

Bardolino: Veneto. Ruby red, dry, slightly bitter.

Barolo: Piemonte. This is one of the most noble Italian wines. Red, dry, full-bodied.

Bianco di Pitigliano: Tuscany. White, dry, slightly bitter.

Brunello di Montalcino: Tuscany. One of the finest wines. Red, full-bodied, dry, aged for 4 years.

Cabernet: Trentino-Alto Adige, Friuli, Veneto. Red, dry, different qualities available.

Cannonau: Sardinia. Red, dry or sweetish depending on the type.

Capri: Island of Capri. White. Dry fresh taste. Also available in red.

Castel del Monte: Apulia. Also available in white (dry and fresh) rosé (dry and harmonious) and red.

Castelli Romani: Latium. White, red or rosé, but the most common is the white which goes well with all courses of a meal.

Chianti: Tuscany. This red, dry wine is perhaps one of the most famous of the Italian wines, dry, full- bodied and suitable for meat dishes.

Cinque Terre: Liguria. Dry white wine. The "Sciacchetrà" type is sweet, and is suitable for desserts.

Cirò: Calabria. This wine is available in white, red and rosé and is, in all cases a dry, harmonious wine.

Colli Albani: Latium. White, dry, delicate and fruity.

Colli Berici: Veneto. The name which is given to different types of wine some of which are dry, delicate white wines and others which are dry full-bodied wines.

Colli Euganei: Veneto. Available in red and white (which can be dry and sweet) and Moscato (sweet).

Colli Lanuvini: Latium. White, dry and delicate.

Colli del Trasimeno: Umbria. White (harmonious, delicate) or red (dry and harmonious).

Collio: Friuli. Name of different wines including dry whites and full-bodied and aromatic reds.

Dolcetto: Piemonte. Several wines are available which take their name from the area in which they are produced. They are all red, dry and slightly bitter despite their name "dolcetto" meaning sweet.

Erbaluce di Caluso: Piemonte. White. The "caluso Passito" is also available which is a sweet dessert wine.

Est!Est!!Est!!!: Latium. Dry, white and full-bodied.

Falerio: Marche. White, dry and slightly bitter.

Frascati: Latium. Dry, delicate white wine also available in a sparkling wine and a sweet one ("Cannellino").

Gattinara: Piemonte. Red, dry and slightly bitter. Aged for at least four years.

Greco di Tufo: Campania. White, dry, delicate. Also available in a sparkling wine.

Grignolino: Piemonte. Red, dry and pleasantly bitter.

Lambrusco: Emilia-Romagna. Red, sparkling, light; generally dry and sweet.

Locorotondo: Apulia. Dry, delicate white wine. Also available in a sparkling wine.

Malvasia: Various regions. A sweet, harmonious and aromatic dessert wine.

Marino: Latium. Fruity, dry white wine.

Marsala: Sicily. Sweet dessert wine with a high alcohol content. It can be dry or sweet and has a strong, full flavor.

Martina Franca: Apulia. Delicate, dry white wine. Sparkling version also available.

Merlot: Various regions. Red, full-flavored aromatic wine which can be slightly bitter on occasion.

Moscato: Various regions. Sweet, delicate, white dessert wine which is sometimes sparkling white. Liqueur versions are also available and have a higher alcohol content.

Nebbiolo: Piemonte. Full-bodied dry red wine which is about 12% proof.

Nuragus: Sardinia. Slightly bitter dry white wine.

Oltrepò Pavese: Lombardy. Name of several wines and the most well-known of these include Bonarda (fresh, red) and Riesling (dry, white).

Orvieto: Umbria. White wine, dry and sweet versions also available.

Pinot: Friuli and other regions. This is one of the most well-known wines in Italy. It is available in "white", "gray" and "black."

Prosecco di Valdobbiadene: Veneto. Sweet, white wine also available in a sparkling wine.

Sangiovese: Romagna. Dry red wine with a bitter aftertaste.

Soave: Veneto. Medium-bodied dry wine.

Spumante: This is the equivalent of French champagne, even if not of quite the same caliber. Some brands are just as good as their French counterpart. Sweet wines are also available. It is mainly served at the end of a meal, but makes an excellent aperitif or can even be drunk with the meal.

Teroldego: Trentino-Alto Adige. Red, (dry, fruity, light mandarin flavor) or rosé (not as full-bodied).

Trebbiano: Romagna. Dry, white. Sparkling, dry or sweet wines are also available.

Valpolicella: Veneto. Full-bodied or slightly sweet red wine.

Verdicchio di Jesi: Marche. White wine which is dry and has a slightly bitter after taste.

Vermentino di Gallura: Sardinia. Dry, slightly bitter white wine.

Vernaccia: Tuscany. Dry, fresh, bitter white wine.

Vino nobile di Montepulciano: Tuscany. Dry, full-bodied red wine which is aged for a period of two years.

Vin santo: Tuscany. Liqueur, dessert wine which is particularly good with dry pastries such as biscuits.

Italy is not only a great wine producing country but it also has a plentiful supply of fruit and perfumed herbs which provide the basic ingredients for the rich tradition of liqueur production.

The various types of *amaro* are worth mentioning. This is a very aromatic digestive liqueur made with herbs and citrus fruit rind; *grappa* is produced mainly in the Trentino, Veneto and Friuli regions, and is available in different versions, some of which are flavored with fruit.

You can also ask for an *amaro* or the "house" liqueur in restaurants, which are often available in family-run restaurants.

Here is a selection of some liqueurs which are certainly worth trying.

Amaretto di Saronno: Very sweet, mandarin flavored, it is produced in large quantities and is available everywhere. It is very pleasant "on the rocks."

Aurum: Sweet, orange flavored, not very common but has a delicate perfume. It is often used to flavor pastries but it is also excellent drunk straight or with ice.

Centerbe: Very high-proof digestive, very strong and aromatic, it falls into the *amaro* category and is typical of the Abruzzo region.

Grappa: Very high-proof distilled drink with a dry taste. It is produced at both industrial and artisan levels. The artisan product can be found in mountainous areas and there is a wide variety of flavors to choose from, one of the better ones being bilberry.

Limoncino: Sweet liqueur with a very strong lemon flavor. It is a typical product of the Campania region, and in particular of the Amalfi Coast area and is best drunk ice-cold.

Mirto: Typical of Sardinia, strong aroma which comes from the myrtle plant after which it is named and from which it gets its flavor.

Nocino: Digestive liqueur which is made by soaking nuts in alcohol. It is very strong, quite sweet and typical of the Emilia-Romagna region and the Parma area in particular.

Sambuca: Liqueur with a strong aniseed flavor, produced commercially and widely available. In Rome, it is drunk *con la mosca*, that is with a coffee bean in the glass.

Sassolino: Typical of the Modena area, this is a sweet aniseed liqueur which is widely used in making pastries but it is not very common outside Modena.

Strega: Sweet and aromatic liqueur which comes from the Campania region but can be found everywhere as it is produced commercially, excellent on ice-cream.

Vermouth (or Vermut): This is not really a liqueur but more a special wine flavored with lots of herbs, originally from Piemonte but widely available, used as an aperitif or for making cocktails.

Every region boasts a wide variety of cake and pastry specialties, and biscuits in particular. Some of these are worth a mention.

Amaretti: These are biscuits made with almonds, sugar and egg white. They are very light and have a distinctive almond flavor. Particularly good versions of these can be found in Saronno (Lombardy) and Sardinia.

Cannoli: These Sicilian pastries have a special place in the Italian pastry tradition. A crunchy pastry shell is filled with a flavored cream filling called *ricotta*. These can be found in almost all Italian pastry shops, but they are not to be missed in Sicily.

Confetti: The best *confetti* (almonds coated in candied sugar) in the world come from Sulmona, a town in the region of Abruzzo, central Italy. They are available in all sorts of shapes, colors and sizes in addition to the classic white ones. They make perfect presents or souvenirs (little bunches of flowers, butterflies, etc).

Fichi in crocetta: These are a specialty from the Calabria region: they are dried figs on a wooden skewer and filled with walnuts and almonds.

Frutti di marzapane/di Martorana: These are sweets made from marzipan (almond paste), typical of Sicily and made into very realistic fruit shapes.

Gelato (Ice-cream): Italian ice-cream is famous worldwide. It is best to try it in big *gelateria* or ice-cream shops, and especially those which display a sign saying "Produzione propria", meaning made in the shop. Not only is the ice-cream homemade but there is also an endless variety of flavors to choose from, ranging from the more traditional to the more imaginative flavors. It is not a good idea to buy ice- cream in small bars or from the ice-cream vans on the street as the flavor is often not great and there is little variety.

SWEETS AND PASTRIES

Gianduiotti: Delicious chocolates from Turin, but available everywhere, they have a distinctive nutty flavor. The original chocolates are shaped like a long triangle and are covered in gold paper.

Granita: Very refreshing especially in the summer, it is made with crushed ice mixed with coffee or mint syrup. Particularly good in Sicily.

Panforte: Specialty from Siena, it is round and flat in shape and is made from honey, dried candied fruit and spices.

Paste: Pastries can be bought in cake shops throughout Italy, but especially in the central and southern regions. The choice is wide, ranging from the cream filled *bigné* to *cannoli siciliani* and so on. You are more likely to find them freshly made on Saturdays and Sundays given that many people take them home on weekends.

Sfogliatelle ricce: These pastries can be bought in almost all pastry shops but they are originally from Naples and this is the best place to try them. They are made of very fine layers of crunchy pastry and are filled with a soft *ricotta* cream and are coated with sugar.

Spongata: This is similar to *panforte di Siena* but is from the Emilia region and some parts of Lombardy and Liguria. The difference between this and *panforte* is that *spongata* is available exclusively at Christmas time.

Torrone: This long-shaped pastry is made with almonds and walnuts, egg whites and sugar. The most common ones available are those from Cremona (Lombardia), Abruzzo and Sicily, but it is produced in more or less all regions. Some versions are covered in chocolate and can usually be found at Christmas.

There are many products, in addition to wines, cheeses, cold cut meats etc. which are worth trying or buying to take home. The following list includes some of the more important ones.

Aceto balsamico: This balsamic vinegar is a specialty from Modena but is available throughout Italy in all well-supplied shops. It is a high-quality, aromatic vinegar which is suitable for seasoning many dishes.

Bottarga: This is a mixture made from the eggs of some fish (generally mullet or gray mullet) pressed, salted and left to mature for several months. It is shaped like a square salami and is usually eaten as a starter, cut very finely and seasoned with oil and lemon and then served on toasted bread. It is often used to flavor pasta. Other versions of this product are also available based on tuna fish eggs or those of other fish which have a stronger flavor and are not quite as good. It is traditionally a Sardinian specialty but it is widely available. It will last for several months in the refrigerator if it is kept well covered.

Ciccioli: These are small fatty pieces of pig meat which are fried and although they can be quite heavy, they are very tasty. They can be bought in shops selling cold cut meats in different regions: Emilia-Romagna and the name varies from one place to another. For example in Latium they are known as *sfrizzoli*) and in Campania they are known as (*cicoli*). They are eaten as a starter or they are used as an ingredient to make appetizing savory pies and are usually available from autumn to spring.

Focaccia: This is the name given to this very soft pizza bread in some areas which is well seasoned with olive oil. It can be bought in bakeries and the *focaccia* available in Liguria is particularly good.

Gnocchi di patate: Made from a mixture of flour and mashed potatoes rolled into small soft balls, this pasta-type specialty is then served in tomato sauce, meat sauce, or other garnishings.

Grissini: These are long, thin sticks of dry, crunchy bread. They come in many shapes and sizes and can be bought in well-supplied bread shops. They are also mass produced and an example of the more common version can be found in any restaurant as a packet of them is always given along with the bread.

Mostarda: This product is from the Lombardy region and Cremona in particular, and is also found in Veneto. It is a special type of seasoning for boiled meat, and consists of fruit which has been left in a sugar and mustard-based syrup thus giving it a sweet-spicy flavor. It is produced commercially nowadays and is available in shops throughout Italy as a result.

Piadina: This flat pizza bread is typical of the Romagna region and is generally filled with salami and is served hot. It is produced commercially outside the Romagna region which is not as good as the original version.

Porchetta: This is roasted pork whereby the animal is cooked whole and is seasoned strongly with garlic, herbs and pepper. It is very common in Umbria but more so in the Latium region where it is sold in the markets and from vans on the side of the street and is eaten in bread rolls (*panini*).

Tartufi: There are two main areas where this flavorsome tuber is produced: the area of Alba in Piemonte where the highly valued white truffle is to be found, and in the Norcia area in Umbria where black truffles can be found. Fresh tartufo are available for a somewhat limited period from late autumn onwards: if kept in oil or some other way, they can be stored for the rest of the year although the flavor is not quite as good. Given the rarity and prestige of this product, they are expensive, especially the white variety.

Besciamella: This is a creamy sauce made with milk, flour and butter. It is frequently used for pasta dishes and other dishes cooked in the oven.

Cotoletta: This is a cutlet which is covered in breadcrumbs and fried.

Crema per dolci (cream for pastries): This is a cream for pastries which is made from eggs, milk, sugar and sometimes flour; flavored with vanilla, lemon or some other flavoring.

Involtini (roulades): A roll made with slices of meat, cold cut meat, chicken or fillet of fish (but in some cases omelettes or leaves of lettuce) wrapped around a filling.

Pesto alla genovese: This is a sauce made from fresh basil, olive oil, pine nuts, cheese and garlic. It has a strong flavor and is usually used as a pasta sauce but also for adding flavor to soups and rice.

Polenta: This is a thick mixture of corn flour cooked in water. It is either seasoned with cheese or mixed with a meat stew in a rich sauce. It is a dish which is typical of the North of Italy.

Polpette (Meatballs): Meatballs made with minced meat or occasionally with fish or vegetables. They are generally fried.

Ragù: This is a pasta sauce made with minced meat. It is also known as Bolognese sauce. In the southern regions and Campania in particular, *Ragù* can mean a thick tomato sauce in which meat has been cooked and then the meat is generally served separately.

Risotto: This is the traditional Italian way of cooking rice which makes it firm and creamy. In some regions of the North, it is cooked *all'onda*, that, is not completely dry and firm. *Risotto* can be flavored with any type of vegetable, fish or other ingredients. Even though it is part of the northern culinary tradition (Lombardy, Piemonte and the Veneto regions in particular), many variations can be found throughout Italy.

Scaloppine or scaloppe: These are small-sized pieces of meat which are fried in butter and seasoned with wine or other ingredients.

Spezzatino: This dish is composed of large pieces of meat (cut to the size of an apricot) cooked in a sauce and often served with vegetables.

Timballo: This is an elaborate dish which is made of alternate layers of pasta or rice and other ingredients (rissole, eggs etc.). It is cooked in the oven in a mold (sometimes in a puff pastry case) and then it is removed from the mold.

Zabaione: This is a cream made with egg yolks, sugar and wine or liqueur. It is very sweet and is generally served with dry pastries (cakes, biscuits). Sometimes it is served with whipped cream.

The following is a list of terms which you are likely to come across in restaurants throughout Italy and refer to dishes which are made in more or less the same way everywhere.

All'agrodolce: This is the name given to some seasonings which are made with vinegar and sugar.

All'arrabbiata: This is the name generally given to a spicy tomato sauce or dishes made with red hot chili peppers.

In bellavista: Refers to dishes, generally fish or meat, which are ornately decorated for serving.

Bocconcini: These are pieces of meat or other foods which have been cut into small mouthful-sized portions.

Alla bolognese: This term generally refers to pasta dishes which are flavored with a meat and tomato sauce (*ragù*) but when referring to meat-based dishes (a cutlet, for example) the term implies that they are covered with a piece of cooked ham and a piece of cheese.

Alla boscaiola: This refers to a sauce or seasoning for pasta, meat, fowl which is made with mushrooms.

Alla brace: Meat and fish are generally cooked this way which is done over the fire or the barbecue.

Alla buongustaia: This refers to rustic, flavorsome seasonings and sauces but they are not made with any one ingredient in particular.

Alla cacciatora: This generally refers to chicken or rabbit dishes and the recipe varies from one area to another although it is usually made with a tasty tomato sauce.

Alla carrettiera: A term used mainly in the Center and South of Italy and consists of a very simple but flavorsome pasta sauce. The recipe varies from one area to another.

Al cartoccio: This cooking method is suitable for any type of food (ranging from pasta to fruit) and is done by placing the food in an envelope made from tinfoil and cooking it in the oven.

Della casa: This refers to sauces or seasonings made exclusively by the restaurant in question and so it is a good idea to ask the waiter what it is. If the term refers to a wine it implies that it will be served in a carafe.

Alla casalinga: This is another generic term referring to a simple "homemade" sauce or seasoning which is not necessarily made with any one ingredient in particular.

In casseruola: This term refers to a dish which is cooked in a pot over a low heat and in a vegetable based sauce.

Alla contadina: Generic term referring to a sauce or seasoning which is made from full-flavored country ingredients.

Alla crema (with cream): If referring to a savory sauce, it usually has a delicate flavor and is made with cream or a *besciamella* sauce which is made with flour, butter and milk. Sweet creamy sauces are usually made with eggs and milk.

In crosta: This refers to meat, fish or some other type of food which is placed in an envelope of puff pastry or bread and cooked in the oven.

Al dente: This is the term used to identify the right texture of spaghetti or pasta when it has been cooked so that it is chewy and slightly hard.

Alla diavola: Refers to dishes which are strongly seasoned with pepper or red hot chili peppers and are therefore hot and spicy.

Fagottini: Portions of food wrapped around a filling (this can be meat, vegetables, etc.).

Ai ferri: Food cooked under the grill or in a pan used for cooking meat or fish.

Fior di latte: This is the name given to a type of mozzarella cheese but it is also used for some desserts and cream-based ice-cream; a bit like vanilla flavor.

Al gratin: Savory food cooked with a layer of besciamella sauce (mixture of flour, butter and milk) or with breadcrumbs, or meringue which is cooked in the oven until it hardens on the outside in the case of desserts and cakes.

Alla griglia: Refers to food cooked on the grill, usually meat or fish but also some vegetables and means the same thing as *ai ferri*.

Mare-monti: Term referring to pasta, rice or crepes which are served with mushrooms and prawns.

Alla marinara: Seafood or anchovies used as seasoning for pasta or rice dishes. It is also the name of a pizza made with tomato, garlic and oregano.

Alla mugnaia: Fish cooked in butter and seasoned with lemon.

Dell'orto: This is a dish made with one or more types of vegetables.

Alla paesana: Generic term referring to dishes which are typical of country cooking and are very tasty.

Alla parmigiana: This term is used for dishes cooked in different ways but all of which are made with a generous helping of Parmesan cheese.

Pasticcio: Rich foods such as pasta, meat, vegetables, etc. covered in a *besciamella* sauce (like white sauce, made with flour, butter and milk) and other ingredients and then cooked in the oven.

Alla pescatora: Pasta or rice with seafood or fish added.

Alla pizzaiola: Refers to meat dishes in general which are cooked with tomato and oregano and occasionally covered with mozzarella.

Al sangue: This is the term used for *rare* when referring to the degree to which meat is cooked as it is still quite red in color.

Trifolati: This is a method of cooking mushrooms or other vegetables in a pan with oil, garlic and parsley.

In umido: This method of cooking is suitable for meat, fish and vegetables and is done in a pan over a low heat in a tomato-based sauce.

Alla valdostana: Cutlets or small pieces of meat fried in butter and seasoned with lemon, covered with a layer of cheese (and sometimes a piece of cooked ham) which is then cooked in the oven.

Vegetariano (or del vegetariano): Refers to a wide variety of vegetarian or vegetable-based dishes made without meat, fish or salami.

Even if the following dishes can be traditionally associated with the area in which they originated, they can be found throughout Italy and have now become part of the country's gastronomic repertoire.

Some of these dishes are better or differ slightly from the original recipe from one area to the next and such cases will be referred to. The name of the dishes is also written in brackets in English and they are listed in alphabetical order.

Several dishes have more than one name and in these cases, the second name will be listed along side the first (for example, Calamari ripieni/imbottiti). Before describing the dish, its position on the menu will be indicated, whether it is a starter, or a first and so on.

Affettati misti (Selection of cold cut meats): Starter. This consists of at least three different types of cold meats such as salami, raw ham, etc. which is generally served with olives and pickled vegetables.

Affogato: Dessert. This is ice-cream served in a glass which is "drowned" or covered in strong coffee or a liqueur.

Agnello arrosto (Roast lamb): Main course. Leg or shoulder of lamb which is seasoned with garlic, rosemary and other herbs.

Amatriciana, pasta alla: Pasta. Usually made with *bucatini* (like spaghetti but tube-shaped), in a tomato sauce with small cubes of bacon and garnished with grated Pecorino cheese. It is more common of the central regions and has a strong flavor which is sometimes spicy.

Anguilla arrosto (or alla griglia) (Roast or grilled eel): Main course. This fish is traditionally eaten throughout Italy at Christmas, and during the rest of the year it is only found in the area around the river Po. It is a fatty fish but is light when grilled or roasted. It is served cut into pieces and is cooked with plenty of herbs (especially dill) and has a distinctive flavor.

Anguilla in umido (Eel cooked in a tomato sauce): Main Course. This dish, eel cooked in a tomato sauce, is typical of the Campania region. In Emilia-Romagna and Veneto, the sauce is clearer and is made with a variety of vegetables (celery, carrots, onions). Both dishes have a distinctive flavor.

Arancini di riso (Rice dish): Starter. Very common in Sicily but is also available in many other regions. This is like a big hamburger-shaped rice cake, covered in breadcrumbs, fried and filled with *ragù* (see the section on "Basics").They are easier to find in shops selling roast meats and chicken, etc. (*rosticceria*) than in restaurants.

Arrabbiata, penne alla: Pasta. Specialty originally from the central regions but is available everywhere. It consists of tubular shaped pasta in a simple tomato sauce with red hot chili peppers to make it spicy. It is generally spicier in the central and southern regions.

Arrosto (Roast): Main course. Generally pork or veal, but it can also be beef or another type of meat (usually always specified). It is served finely sliced and covered in gravy.

Arrosto misto di pesce/Pesce arrosto (Mix of baked fish/baked fish): Main course. This dish is often found in restaurants which specialize in fish and usually consists of a whole fish, a few large prawns and cuttle fish, all cooked under the grill.

Arrosto in crosta (Roast meat in pastry): Main course. The roast meat is cooked in a pastry case made with bread dough or another type of pastry and it is then served sliced with its crunchy exterior.

Asparagi alla Bismark (Asparagus cooked Bismark style): Main course. Asparagus boiled and served with an egg which has been fried in butter.

Asparagi, involtini di (Stuffed asparagus): Boiled asparagus, rolled in slices of ham and cooked in the oven.

Babà: Dessert. This is a bit like a sponge cake made with yeast which is then covered with a rum syrup. It is originally from Naples and this is the best place to try it although it can be found in cake shops throughout Italy.

Baccalà fritto (Fried cod): Main course. Cod which has been preserved in salt is known as *baccalà*. It is desalinated, softened and then cooked. First the fish is dipped in a mixture of flour, water, a little oil and salt and then it is fried.

Bavarese: Dessert. This is a pudding made with whipped cream or fresh and light puréed fruit.

Bistecca alla fiorentina (Steak cooked Florentine style): Main course. This is a big steak cooked rare. It is best to try it in Tuscany as the meat there is the most suitable.

Bollito misto (Mixture of boiled meat): Main course. This dish consists of various different quality meats: usually beef, veal and hen. Although this dish is traditionally from the Piemonte, Lombardy and Emiliana regions, it is available almost everywhere. It is usually served with a *salsa verde* or green sauce made from olive oil, parsley and the soft doughy center of bread.

Boscaiola, pasta alla: Pasta. This is generally egg pasta which is flavored with a sauce of mushrooms, peas and cream and has a very subtle flavor. There is another version of the sauce with a stronger flavor which is made from mushrooms and tomato sauce.

Brasato al vino (Braised beef cooked in wine): Main course. This dish is generally made with beef cooked in lots of vegetables, red wine and spices which is then served sliced and doused in gravy. The most famous version is the one from Piemonte which is cooked in Barolo wine.

Bresaola: Starter. This cold cut meat is served sliced, seasoned with olive oil, lemon, salt, pepper and sometimes Parmesan cheese. The best place to try this is high in the vales of Lombardy where it originated.

Bresaola, involtini di (Stuffed Bresaola meat): Starter. Slices of Bresaola filled with fresh, creamy cheese and aromatic herbs.

Broccoli, pasta e: Pasta. This dish is common in the central and southern regions and consists of pasta and green broccoli which have been stirred in a pan with olive oil, garlic and red hot chili peppers. It is quite spicy. A soup version also exists which is made with more or less the same ingredients.

Brodetto di pesce (Fish soup): First course. This dish, which can be found in coastal areas, is composed of quite a watery fish soup although the consistency varies from one area to the next. It always contains different types of fish and shellfish. It is seasoned with some fried garlic and the olive oil in which it is cooked and garnished with a slice of toasted bread. In the central and southern regions it is slightly spicy.

Bruschetta: Starter. This is simply a slice of toasted bread, rubbed with a piece of garlic and seasoned with olive oil and oregano or else raw tomatoes, oil and garlic. It is more typical of the central regions and is particularly good in Latium and Tuscany.

Calamari ripieni/imbottiti (Stuffed squid): Main course. The squid are stuffed with a mixture of breadcrumbs, egg, garlic and other ingredients and then cooked in a tomato and oil sauce. This dish can be found in southern regions and in Liguria and can vary slightly from one region to another.

Calzoni: Starter. This is like a pizza which has been folded in half and filled with cheese and cold meats or vegetables. It is then either fried or cooked in the oven. They can mainly be found in pizzerias and are particularly good in the Campania region.

Cannelloni: Pasta/first course. Tubular shaped egg pasta which is filled with meat or ricotta (cottage cheese made with skimmed milk) and spinach, and cooked in a tomato and *besciamella* or white sauce (see section on "Basics"), plenty of Parmesan cheese and then cooked in the oven. It has a subtle flavor in northern regions and a stronger flavor in the central and southern regions.

Cappelletti/Tortellini/Agnolini in brodo: Pasta. Egg pasta filled with meat and served in a meat broth. It is excellent in Emilia-Romagna and the lower part of the Lombardy region where it is easier to find homemade versions.

Caprese: Starter or main course. Fresh salad which consists of slices of tomato and mozzarella cheese, seasoned with olive oil and fresh basil. It is excellent in Campania if the mozzarella is made with buffalo milk.

Capretto al forno (Kid meat cooked in the oven): Main course. Available at Easter time and difficult to find at other times of the year. This tender meat is seasoned with aromatic herbs and sometimes tomatoes, onions and potatoes are added (especially in the southern regions).

Carbonara, pasta alla: Pasta. Spaghetti or *bucatini* (tubular spaghetti), seasoned with a creamy mixture of egg, Parmesan cheese and fried bacon cubes in its oil plus freshly ground black pepper. It is full flavored and slightly spicy (depending on the quantity of pepper). It's well worth trying in the Latium region.

Carpaccio: Starter. Very lean beef which is cut into fine slices, served raw and seasoned with olive oil, pepper, lemon juice, flakes of Parmesan cheese and sometimes raw mushrooms or other ingredients.

Carpione di pesce/pesce in carpione (Marinated fish): Starter. This is generally fresh water fish which has been fried and marinated in a vinegar-based sauce. Strong flavor.

Cartoccio, pasta al: Pasta/first course. This is spaghetti in a tomato and seafood sauce which is placed in a tinfoil envelope and put in the oven.

Ceci, Pasta e: Pasta. Thick and full-flavored soup made with oil, garlic, a little tomato and sometimes rosemary. Excellent in Tuscany but also in central and southern Italy.

Coniglio alla cacciatora (Rabbit): Main course. Rabbit stew cooked in a pot with fried onions, wine and sometimes mushrooms and tomatoes.

Coniglio alle olive (Rabbit with olives): Main course. The rabbit is cut into pieces and cooked in a pot with tomatoes, olives, garlic and wine. The tomatoes are omitted in some versions but, whatever way it is cooked, it always has a great flavor. It is well worth trying in Liguria.

Costolette/Cotolette alla milanese (Cutlets/chops cooked Milanese style): Main course. Chops or cutlets dipped in breadcrumbs and fried, usually in butter.

Costolette/cotolette alla bolognese (Cutlets/chops cooked Bolognese style): Main course. Similar to the above recipe except for the addition of a piece of raw ham and cheese on the top.

Cozze alla marinara/Sauté di cozze (Sautéed mussels): Starter. The mussels are flavored with a mixture of oil, garlic and parsley and are served with their juices.

Crema fritta (Fried cream): Dessert. These are very soft pancakes, specialties of the various regions of north and central Italy. Even though they are sweet, they are served with the *fritto misto* (different fried foods-see below) and sometimes with vegetables as well. There is also a savory version made with cheese. They are best in the Emilia and Lombardy regions.

Crostata alla ricotta (Pastry filled with ricotta): Dessert. This is a short crust pastry pie filled with a ricotta (cottage cheese made with skimmed milk) soft cream, with candied fruit and raisins. It is worth trying in Lazio, Umbria and the Marche regions.

Crostata di frutta (Fruit tart): Dessert. Short crust pastry tart covered in cream, fresh fruit and gelatine. This is one of the most common desserts.

Crostini: Starter. These are slices of toasted bread, the topping of which varies from region to region. Chicken liver is particularly common in Tuscany while mozzarella and anchovies are typical of the Lazio region.

Fagioli con le cotiche (Beans with pig rind): Main course. Flavorsome, filling country dish which can be found in some trattorias (inns) in the countryside. The beans are cooked together with the pig rind, tomatoes and other ingredients.

Fagioli, Pasta e: Pasta. Very tasty country soup. It is a good idea to add a drop of olive oil before eating it.

Fegato alla veneta/alla veneziana (Liver cooked Veneto style): Thin slices of veal liver cooked in a pot with lots of onion. Even though you can find this dish in most places, it is best in the Veneto region where it originated.

Fettuccine ai piselli: Pasta/first course. Pasta with cream, peas and ham. This dish has a delicate flavor and is particularly good in Lazio.

Filetto al pepe verde (Fillet with green pepper): Main course. This is a fillet of beef cooked in butter and covered with a sauce made from cream, brandy, mustard and green pepper. It has a delicate and aromatic flavor.

Fiori di zucca fritti/Frittelle di fiori di zucca (Fried courgette flowers): Starter. The delicate flowers of the courgette plant are dipped in batter and deep-fried. They are worth trying in Lazio and in Liguria where they are filled with an anchovy mixture.

Fonduta (Fondue/melted cheese with cream and eggs): Starter. In Italy this usually refers to hot creamy *fontina* cheese (cheese from the Aosta region) in which pieces of bread are dipped or else used for seasoning pasta, rice or other dishes. It is worth trying in Piemonte where white truffles are added for extra flavor. The cheese used gives it a distinctive flavor.

Fragole con panna (Strawberries with cream): Dessert. This dessert is a typical spring dish and consists of a fruit salad of strawberries with sugar and sometimes liqueur and whipped cream. A variation of this is *fragole al limone* or strawberries which have been covered in sugar and some lemon juice.

Fritto misto (Mixed fry): Starter or main course. This is a mixture of different fried foods including some vegetables, meat or giblets, rice or potato cakes etc. Its ingredients vary from one region to the next and often it is served with a few sweet pancakes. Try this dish in Piemonte.

Fritto misto di mare/di pesce (Mix of fried fish): Main course usually consisting of king-sized prawns and squid and sometimes small fish, which have been dipped in batter and fried.

Funghi, Pasta ai (Pasta with mushrooms): Pasta/ first course. It is easy to find dishes made with fresh mushrooms from the woods in restaurants near the hills and mountains towards the end of the summer. The best dishes are those made with boletus or *porcini* mushrooms, but other tasty varieties include *chiodini*, *finferli* and many others. They are really worth tasting in the Trentino-Alto Adige, Piemonte and Veneto regions.

Gnocchi alla bava: Pasta/first course. Type of pasta made with a mixture of basic pasta ingredients and mashed potato, seasoned with *fonduta* (see above). Delicate flavor.

Gnocchi alla romana: Pasta/first course. Small semolino shapes cooked in milk, seasoned with butter and cheese and then put in the oven. Soft in texture and delicately flavored, this is a specialty of the Latium region but different versions are available elsewhere.

Insalata di mare (Seafood salad): Starter. Cold dish made from squid, prawns, etc. which are boiled and then seasoned with oil, parsley, lemon.

Insalata di riso (Rice salad): Starter or first course. Boiled rice served cold, seasoned with oil, vegetables, tuna fish and other chopped ingredients. This is a typical fresh summer dish and is rarely spicy.

Involtini (Stuffed meat rolls): Main course. Meat rolls (or fish in some cases) which are filled with vegetables or other ingredients. There is an infinite variety to choose from but the more common ones (which are also known as *Uccelli scappati* or *Messicani*) are made with veal with a cheese and ham filling and are cooked in a pot, sometimes in a tomato sauce.

Lasagne: Pasta/first course. This dish is known as *Pasticcio* in some regions and even though it varies from one region to the next, it is basically made of several layers of egg pasta with a sauce between each layer and then placed in the oven. The most common version is the *bolognese* which is best in the Emilia-Romagna region. Here it is made with a *ragù* and *besciamella* sauce (see section on "Basics") and has a delicate but tasty flavor. In southern regions, this is substituted with a tomato sauce which is enriched with meat balls, boiled eggs, cheese and other ingredients.

Lenticchie, Zuppa di (Lentil soup): First course. Thick, tasty vegetable soup, seasoned with olive oil, some tomato and some Pecorino or Parmesan cheese. Excellent in Tuscany and throughout the central and southern regions.

Maccheroni/Pasta ai 4 formaggi (Pasta with four cheeses): Pasta/first course. The pasta is seasoned with butter, Parmesan, Gorgonzola, Mozzarella and Fontina or other cheeses, resulting in a creamy and delicately flavored dish.

Macedonia (Fruit salad): Dessert. Salad of fresh fruit which is seasoned with sugar and lemon. It is also served with ice-cream upon request.

Melanzane al funghetto (Eggplants): Side serving. Eggplants cut into small pieces and cooked in oil, parsley, garlic and sometimes with a little bit of tomato. Appetizing but not usually spicy. Recommended in the Campania region.

Melanzane alla parmigiana (Eggplant in Parmesan cheese): Side serving or main course. Slices of eggplant which have been fried and alternated with layers of tomato sauce and Parmesan cheese and then cooked in the oven. It is served hot or warm. In the North it is known as *Parmigiana di melanzane* (see below).

Melanzane grigliate (Grilled eggplants): Starter or side serving. Slices of grilled eggplant seasoned with oil, garlic and parsley. They are often served as part of a selection of mixed starters.

Melanzane ripiene (Stuffed eggplants): Starter. The vegetable is cut in half and emptied. It is then stuffed with a mixture of breadcrumbs, Parmesan cheese, herbs and oil and then cooked in the oven. It is eaten warm or cold and is more common in the southern regions.

Melone al Porto (Melon with Port): Dessert. The fruit is cut in half and soaked in Port wine. This is a fresh summer dish.

Millefoglie: Dessert. Cake made with very light puff pastry and filled with cream.

Minestrone (Soup): First course. This is a mixed vegetable soup containing rice or pasta. It is usually served thick and seasoned with olive oil. The version to be found in Liguria is very appetizing and has some *pesto alla genovese* added (see section on "Basics").

Mozzarella in carrozza: Starter. This is a sandwich filled with mozzarella cheese and sometimes ham or anchovies, covered in breadcrumbs and fried. It is more commonly available in pizzerias than in restaurants and is particularly good in the Campania region.

Mozzarella fritta (Fried mozzarella): Starter. The cheese which has been cut into pieces is covered in breadcrumbs or dipped in a batter and then fried. Worth trying in Rome.

Ossibuchi: Main course. These are slices of veal taken from the shinbone and include a piece of the bone and its marrow. They are usually cooked in a rich tomato and mushroom sauce and sometimes served with polenta (see "Basics" section) in the North.

Panna cotta (Cooked cream): Dessert. This is a cold, soft pudding made almost exclusively of cream, milk and sugar. It is served with a fruit sauce or with caramel.

Panzerotti: Starter. These are little pasta rounds which have been filled and closed over and vary depending on the region (often mozzarella and tomato) and are cooked in the oven.

Parmigiana di melanzane (Eggplants and Parmesan cheese): Side serving or main course. This is a rich dish which is common in the southern regions. It consists of layers of fried eggplant alternated with a tomato sauce, mozzarella cheese, boiled eggs, Parmesan cheese and other ingredients and it is then cooked in the oven. It is a very appetizing dish and generally not spicy.

Pasta al forno (Pasta cooked in the oven): Pasta/ first course.Very similar to lasagne (see above). This dish is tasty and the rich ingredients include meat and cheese.

Pasta allo scoglio: Pasta/first course. Usually spaghetti with different shellfish cooked in a tomato sauce. It is particularly good in the Campania and Latium regions.

Pasticcio di maccheroni: Pasta/first course. This is a very filling pasta dish with tomato sauce and chicken liver or *ragù* (see "Basics" section) and other ingredients and it is then put in the oven. In other regions, the pasta is cooked in a puff pastry.

Peperonata: Side serving. Tasty dish made from peppers cooked in a pot with oil, onions and tomato.

Peperoni arrostiti (Roast peppers): Starter or side serving. The peppers are roasted, cut into strips and then seasoned with oil, garlic and parsley. They can be found in the central and southern regions especially.

Pesce al cartoccio: Main course. Cooking method for quite large fish which are cooked in the oven in a tinfoil case and flavored with herbs.

Piccata/Scaloppina al Marsala: Main course. Thin slices of veal cooked in a pan and flavored with Marsala (wine) and served in a thick sauce. In other versions, the meat is flavored with white wine and lemon juice. This dish has a delicate flavor.

Pizza: Main course. Thin, soft bread base topped with tomato and other ingredients and baked. Best in a wood-fire oven.

Pizza capricciosa: Tomato and mushrooms, artichokes and boiled egg.

Pizza Margherita: This is the simplest version, flavored with tomato, mozzarella cheese and fresh basil.

Pizza napoletana: With mozzarella, tomato and anchovies.

Pizza 4 stagioni (4 seasons): With tomato, mushrooms, mussels, salami and ham.

Pollo alla cacciatora: Main course. The chicken is cut into pieces and cooked in a pot with a tasty sauce made from tomato, mushrooms and herbs. It is particularly good in the regions of Emilia-Romagna, Tuscany and the Marche.

Pollo alla diavola: Main course. The chicken is cut in half, seasoned with lots of pepper and cooked under the grill. It is quite spicy and is worth trying in Tuscany.

Pollo alla Marengo: Main course. Chicken cooked in tomato and garnished with a fried egg, breadcrumbs and some prawns. It is usually more common in Piemonte and Lombardy.

Polipi/Polipetti affogati: Main course. Shellfish cooked in a tasty tomato sauce. Good in the Campania region.

Profiteroles: Dessert. Despite the French name, this dessert is very common in Italy. These are little cream puffs filled with cream and covered in chocolate.

Prosciutto e melone (Ham and melon): Starter. This is a very common starter during the summer: cool and simple, it consists of slices of raw ham (usually sweet) and cantaloupe melon served on a plate.

Radicchio di Treviso alla griglia: Side serving. This chicory from Treviso, also known as *trevisana* or *radicchio rosso* (red chicory), is a slightly bitter tasting lettuce which is grilled and seasoned with oil.

Ravioli: Pasta. Fresh, square-shaped egg pasta, usually filled with meat but often with *ricotta* (like cottage cheese made with skimmed milk) and other ingredients. They are usually flavored with butter or else a tomato sauce.

Risotto agli scampi: First course. Rice with a delicate, creamy pink colored sauce (due to tomatoes) made with shellfish. The fish flavor is very weak.

Risotto ai funghi: First course. This dish is excellent if made with fresh *porcini* mushrooms and it is advisable to try it when they are in season (late summer) and in areas near the mountains (Piemonte, Veneto, Trentino, etc.).

Risotto alla milanese: First course. This rice is flavored and colored by saffron and has a delicate and slightly spicy flavor. It is sometimes served with meat dishes, such as *ossibuchi*. Naturally it is best in its city of origin, Milan.

Risotto alla pescatora: First course. Tasty dish where the rice is cooked in a tomato sauce and a mix of shellfish.

Risotto al nero di seppia: First course. The rice is flavored with the black ink and finely cut pieces of cuttlefish.

Salsicce con patate (Sausage with potatoes): Main course. Classic country dish made with a mixture of potato and sausage cooked in the oven. It can be more or less spicy depending on the sausage.

Scaloppine: Main course. See *Piccata* above.

Semifreddo: Dessert. Very similar to ice-cream, flavored with biscuits, liqueur or other ingredients.

Sorbetto: Dessert. This is also similar to ice-cream but it is not as creamy and is generally fruit-based. It is served between courses in the more elegant restaurants to "clean" ones palate. The lemon flavored sorbetto is very refreshing.

Spaghetti aglio, olio e peperoncino: Pasta. Pasta with olive oil, garlic and red hot chili peppers. Quite spicy. Recommended in the Lazio region.

Spaghetti alla carbonara: See above under *Carbonara*.

Spaghetti alle vongole (Spaghetti with clams): Pasta. There are two versions of this dish: one with tomato where the clam is removed from its shell and the other version which is *in bianco* where the clams are bigger and are served in their shells and there are no tomatoes. Both dishes are very appetizing as they are seasoned with garlic and olive oil and red hot chili peppers on occasion. They are recommended in the Campania region and coastal areas.

Supplì: Starter. This is a tomato flavored rice ball with a piece of mozzarella cheese in the center rolled in breadcrumbs and then deep fried. It is more common in pizzerias and shops selling roast meat etc. (*rosticcerie*), especially in Latium.

Tiramisù: Dessert. Even if this is a fairly recent dessert, it has been hugely successful and is available in restaurants throughout Italy. This fresh cold dessert consists of a cream base of *mascarpone* (see "Typical Products" section) and egg which is layered alternately with biscuits which have been soaked in coffee. It is delicious but quite heavy.

Torta salata/rustica: Starter. This is a type of pizza or quiche with filling and there are many different varieties. The most common fillings are spinach or ham and cheese.

Trippa (Tripe): Main course. Every region has its own recipe, but these cows' intestines are usually cooked with lots of herbs, vegetables, tomato and sometimes grated cheese. In all cases it is a filling and tasty country dish.

Vitello tonnato (Veal with tuna): Starter. Cold dish of lean boiled meat, cut into thin slices and covered with a sauce of tuna fish and mayonnaise. It is delicate and fresh and is particularly good in Piemonte.

Zuccotto: Dessert. This dome-shaped dessert consists of sponge cake which has been soaked in liqueur and filled with frozen cream. Particularly good in the area around Florence.

Zuppa di pesce (Fish soup): First course. This soup is made with several types of fish and olive oil and tomatoes. It is usually spicier in the southern regions.

Zuppa inglese: Dessert. Despite the name this is an Italian dessert made with layers of chocolate and egg cream alternated with biscuits which have been soaked in liqueur and strong coffee. It is served cold or, in some cases, hot and covered in meringue.

Much more space would be needed if all the regional dishes and their variations were to be listed here. We will limit ourselves to offering a fairly comprehensive guide to the most typical dishes of each region. A brief description of each region's cooking will also be included.

We will also indicate the position of the dish on the menu as indicated in the section on "National dishes" in addition to its main ingredients.

PIEMONTE AND VALLE D'AOSTA

The wine and cheese in these regions are excellent and provide the basis for some great recipes. Rice, which is produced in Piemonte, is another one of the basic ingredients. White truffle is used in almost all of the more elegant dishes, while meat and fresh water fish from the lakes of the region are used in the more basic dishes as well as mushrooms from the alpine forests, when in season.

Many of these regional dishes are available nationally and have been included in the section on "National dishes."

Antipasto di verdure: Starter. Peppers and other vegetables which are preserved in oil, often homemade.

Bagna caoda: Starter. This is a very strong-flavored sauce made with garlic or anchovies and is used for dipping raw vegetables in.

Bonet: Dessert. Soft chocolate pudding.

Brasato al Barolo (Braised beef): Main course. Superb dish of meat simmered in this excellent Piemontese wine.

Carne all'albese: Starter or main course. Very lean raw beef, sliced and marinated in a mixture of oil, salt, pepper and and scales of truffle.

Paniscia/Panissa: First course. Heavy dish of rice, beans and pork.

Polenta concia: Main course. The polenta (like semolina) is seasoned with butter and cheese (including the famous *fontina* cheese from the Valle d'Aosta).

Rostone: Main course. Very delicately flavored roast beef, served in a cream and truffle sauce.

Tajarin: Pasta/first course. Thin layers of egg pasta flavored with melted butter and truffle.

Torta Gianduia: Dessert. Delicious nut and chocolate cake.

LIGURIA

Ligurian cooking is based on fish, herbs and vegetables and its excellent olive oil. Many dishes, from soup to lasagne are often flavored with *pesto alla genovese* (See "Basics" section). Rabbit meat is commonly used. This is one of the lightest cuisines in Italy.

Cappon magro: Starter or main course. Rich salad based on many different types of fish and shellfish, vegetables, mushrooms and seasoned with a very tasty dressing.

Cima alla genovese: Main course. One of the few typical meat (bovine) dishes. It consists of a "pocket" of meat filled with giblets, boiled and served sliced.

Farinata: Starter. This is a type of pizza made with chick-pea flour and is very appetizing.

Pansotti al pesto di noci: Pasta/first course. Egg pasta filled with vegetables and ricotta (like cottage cheese made with skimmed milk) and seasoned with a sauce of sliced walnuts, cream, oil and cheese. Very delicate flavor.

Torta Pasqualina: Starter. Very delicately flavored quiche filled with spinach, ricotta (like cottage cheese made with skimmed milk), and egg. There are versions which vary from the original but are just as good, such as one with artichoke filling.

Trenette al pesto: Pasta/first course. Pasta with this strong-flavored basil sauce which is typical of this region.

LOMBARDY

The cuisine in this region tends to vary from one province to the next. It is meat and vegetable-based but there are many dishes made with the fresh water fish from the lakes in the region. Butter is the main ingredient used for seasoning and flavoring, rice is the main ingredient used in the first courses. The many cheeses produced in the area are used in several of the recipes.

Busecca: First course. Heavy but very tasty dish made from tripe and beans.

Cassoeula: Main course. This is a typical country winter dish based on pork, sausage and savoy cabbage cooked in a tomato sauce. Not advisable if you have a delicate stomach!

Ossibuchi in gremolada: Main course. This meat dish is also known as *Ossibuchi alla milanese* and is distinguished by the addition of a strong-flavored mixture of crushed garlic, parsley and lemon rind.

Pizzoccheri alla valtellinese: Pasta/first course. This pasta, a bit like *tagliatelle*, is made with dark flour and is seasoned with butter, cheese and vegetables.

Polenta e osei: Main course. The polenta (like semolina) is served with roast fowl and its gravy.

Riso alla pilota: First course. This dish, typical of Mantova, consists of rice and a sausage meat sauce.

Risotto alla certosina: First course. Rich, rice-based dish with frogs, prawns, mushrooms and peas. Very delicate.

Stufato/Stracotto: Main course. Bovine meat cooked slowly in vegetables, wine and broth until it becomes very tender. It is served in its sauce.

Torta sbrisolona: Dessert. This is a crunchy, crumbly cake with cream or *zabaione* (See "Basics" section).

Tortelli di zucca: Pasta/first course. Egg pasta with a sweet-flavored filling of cooked, stewed pumpkin. They are seasoned with butter and grated cheese.

VENETO

This region includes part of the coast, mountains and lowlands and its cuisine reflects this geographic diversity. *Polenta* (see "Basics" section) is one of the basic ingredients. Fish and shellfish, and in particular *granseole* (crab), *cape sante* (scallops) and *peoci* (mussels) are the basic ingredients used in the areas around the coast and lakes. In the lowlands many of the recipes are made with poultry (chicken, turkey) which are bred in the area. Some of the best vegetables are also cultivated in this area such as asparagus from Bassano and chicory from Treviso.

Baccalà mantecato: Main course. Delicate cod dish which is cooked, broken into pieces and added to oil and herbs resulting in a kind of cream. Usually served with a type of toasted *polenta*.

Bigoli in salsa: Pasta/first course. *Bigoli* are a type of spaghetti flavored with an appetizing sauce made from onions and anchovies.

Bollito con salsa pearà: Main course. Boiled meat which is served with a strong-flavored sauce of breadcrumbs, cheese, broth and quite a lot of pepper.

Pinza: Dessert. This is a cake made with yellow flour, raisins and pine nuts.

Risi e bisi: First course. Thick rice and pea soup, appetizing but subtle flavor.

Tacchino alla melagrana: Main course. Roast turkey flavored with the turkey's liver and pomegranate seeds.

TRENTINO-ALTO ADIGE

The cuisine is quite similar in these two areas; the basic ingredients include pork, sausages, cheese and polenta. Dry pasta (maccheroni, spaghetti, etc.) is used in most of the restaurants but this is only a recent introduction and is not in line with the tradition of the area. The influence of Austrian cuisine is evident in Alto Adige.

Canederli: First course. Large balls of bread flavored with herbs and *speck* (See section on "Cold cut meats"), served in a meat broth or else dry but covered in melted butter.

Orzetto: First course. Soup of barley, potatoes and some vegetables, flavored with pieces of bacon.

Smacafam: Main course. Dark colored polenta, seasoned with lard and sausage. Not for delicate stomachs!

Strangolapreti: Pasta/first course. Pasta with bread and spinach, usually flavored with melted butter and sage. Delicate flavor.

Stinco di maiale: This cut of pork which comes from the shin bone, is found almost exclusively in this region. It is appetizing when roasted and is worth a try.

Strudel di mele (Apple strudel): Dessert. This dessert is originally from Austria but it is one of the most typical dishes of the region and is made with locally grown apples.

Trota salmonata (Trout): Main course. The flesh of this very delicate fresh water fish is pink in color and is usually grilled or fried in butter.

Zelten: Dessert. Rich dessert which is eaten at Christmas and is made with dried fruit.

FRIULI-VENEZIA GIULIA

The cuisine in this region is quite economical and is based on pork and beans as well as polenta. Excellent wine, cold cut meats and cheese production.

Cialzons: Pasta/first course. Type of ravioli with a bitter sweet filling, usually potatoes. They are seasoned with melted butter and local cheese.

Frico: Main course. Local cheese which is sliced and fried in a pan on its own or with onions.

Gubana: Dessert. Dessert made with puff pastry and dried fruit.

Musetto e brovade: Main course. Filling dish made from a type of cooked salami and turnips. Very tasty.

Presnitz: Dessert. Rich dessert made with dried fruit.

EMILIA-ROMAGNA

The cooking in this region is one of the richest in the country, based on the abundant and varied cold cut meat production and the excellent Parmigiano Reggiano (Parmesan) cheese and finally the many pasta dishes made with egg pasta. There are many meat-based dishes and the fish is excellent in the coastal part of the region. The bread is also excellent throughout. The most famous dishes from the Emilia region have been dealt with in the section on "National dishes."

Bomba di riso: First course. This is a rich rice pie with a pigeon meat filling.

Calzagatti: First course. This is a soft polenta flavored with a tomato, beans and bacon sauce.

Cotechino in camicia: Main course. The *cotechino*, which is a type of cooked sausage, is the filling for a roast meat and is often cooked in Lambrusco, a red wine from the region.

Erbazzone: Starter. Appetizing quiche which has a filling of herbs, spinach and ricotta between two layers of pastry.

Gnocco fritto: Starter. Small, crunchy rolls of pasta served with local cold cut meats and sparkling Lambrusco wine.

Passatelli: First course. Soft little dumplings made with potato or semolina and breadcrumbs and cheese served in a meat broth.

Scaloppine alla bolognese: Main course. Slices of turkey or veal cooked in butter, then covered in raw ham or mortadella (see section on "Cold cut meats") and fresh Parmesan cheese and placed briefly in the oven.

Torta di riso/degli addobbi (rice cake): Dessert. This is a soft cake which is traditional in Bologna and is made from rice cooked in milk.

Tortelli verdi: Pasta/first course. Large pieces of square-shaped egg pasta, filled with spinach and cheese, flavored with butter and Parmesan cheese.

Tuscany

This is one of the most varied regional cuisines in the country: from the appetizing fish dishes along the coast, to the superb meat from the Maremma region, and the tasty soups which can be found throughout the area. The dishes are fairly simple although each dish is enriched by the excellent olive oil and one of the excellent wines of the region to accompany it.

Acquacotta: First course. Simple and appetizing soup made from peppers and other vegetables, eggs and toasted bread. Boletus mushrooms are also added when in season.

Arista: Main course. Tender roast pork with sage, garlic and rosemary.

Cacciucco: First course. Very flavorsome fish soup from Livorno, with tomato.

Castagnaccio: Dessert. Flat and compact cake made from chestnut flour, sprinkled with raisins and pine nuts. It is not very sweet.

Crostini di milza: Starter. Slices of toasted bread spread with a veal spleen paté.

Fagioli al fiasco: Vegetables. White beans cooked in a special way and seasoned with oil, garlic and sage.

Fagioli all'uccelletto: Vegetables. Similar to the above recipe but with plenty of tomato sauce added.

Panzanella: Starter. Cold and simple salad made from bread which has been soaked in water and mixed with tomatoes, raw onions, herbs and vinegar.

Pappa al pomodoro (Bread soup with tomatoes): First course. Tomato-based soup which can be eaten either hot or cold, adding a little oil.

Pappardelle alla lepre: Pasta/first course. Long ribbons of egg pasta with an aromatic sauce made with hare. It is also common to find the same dish made with rabbit.

Pici: Pasta/first course. Soft spaghtetti with mushrooms.

Ribollita: First course. Simple country soup made from beans and cabbage, seasoned with olive oil.

Triglie alla livornese: Main course. The mullet is browned in oil and garlic and then cooked in a tomato sauce.

Zuppa di farro: First course. This is one of the best of the region's many soups. It is made with an unusual cereal called spelt and beans, flavored with the excellent Tuscan oil. It is thick and tasty.

MARCHE

The cooking along the coast is based on fish while inland it is heavier and well-seasoned.

Brodetto: Fish soup with a distinctive onion flavor. This recipe varies considerably.

Olive all'ascolana: Starter. Large green olives stuffed with a meat filling, covered with breadcrumbs and then deep-fried.

Ravioli all'anconetana: Pasta/first course. Egg pasta which gets its distinctive flavor from its cheese filling, lemon rind and a little sugar. They are cooked and then put in the oven.

Stoccafisso in potacchio: Main course. Dried cod which is cooked in a thick tomato sauce and then put in the oven with potatoes.

Vincisgrassi: Pasta/first course. Rich dish similar to *lasagne* (See section on "National dishes"). Layers of egg pasta are alternated with a sauce of veal giblets, tomato and *besciamella* (See "Basics" section).

UMBRIA

Simple cooking, the main ingredients of which include the very good local oil, the cheeses, black truffle from Norcia and cold cut meats. Many of the main courses are based on wild fowl.

Ciaramicola: Dessert. Traditional Easter dessert made with yeast and decorated with colored sugar-coated almonds.

Pizza al formaggio: Starter. Country quiche made with cheese, egg and ham.

Porchetta alla perugina (Pork): Main course. Whole pig cooked on the spit and seasoned with herbs and garlic.

Spaghetti/Fettuccine al tartufo (Spaghetti with truffle): Pasta/first course. Pasta seasoned with slices of browned truffle.

LATIUM

The Latium cuisine is more country-style cooking which consists of simple pasta dishes and main courses including lamb or giblets, artichokes and almost always garlic. Fish and shellfish dishes are also to be found, and king-sized shrimp which are known as *mazzancolle* are usually grilled.
Rome has somewhat lost its own local traditional dishes and the more generic dishes are available everywhere. It is quite difficult to find restaurants which specialize in Roman cuisine.

Abbacchio a scottadito (Lamb): Main course. Tender lamb cutlets cooked on charcoal.

Abbacchio brodettato (Lamb): Lamb stew served in a sauce made from egg, lemon juice and herbs. Very delicate.

Carciofi alla giudia (Artichokes): Starter or vegetable. Tender artichokes fried in oil and served crisp and whole with their stalk.

Carciofi alla romana (Artichokes): Vegetable. Large cooked artichokes, flavored with garlic and mint.

Coda alla vaccinara (Oxtail): Main course. Appetizing dish made with oxtail in a tomato, celery and vegetable sauce.

Crostino: Starter. Slices of bread which have been cooked in the oven and covered with mozzarella cheese and flavored with an anchovy sauce.

Crostino al prosciutto: Starter. Slices of bread which have been cooked in the oven with ham and mozzarella cheese.

Garofalato di bue (Ox): Main course. Meat which has been simmered with tomatoes, vegetables and cloves which give this dish its distinctive flavor.

Maccheroni alla norcina: Pasta/first course. Pasta with a cream and sausage sauce.

Pollo alla romana (Chicken): Main course. Chicken pieces cooked in a pepper-based sauce.

Pomodori al riso (Tomatoes with rice): First course. Large tomatoes stuffed with rice and cooked in the oven.

Puntarelle all'acciuga: Vegetable. Tasty, crunchy salad, seasoned with a garlic and anchovy-based sauce.

Rigatoni con la pajata: Pasta/first course. Pasta with a sauce made from lambs' intestines.

Saltimbocca alla romana: Main course. Tender, delicate pieces of veal covered in ham and cooked in butter, sage and white wine.

Spaghetti alla checca: Pasta/first course. Superb summer pasta dish with raw tomatoes flavored with garlic and fresh basil.

Spaghetti alla gricia: Pasta/first course. Pasta with fried onions and bacon pieces, grated cheese and pepper.

Spaghetti cacio e pepe: Pasta/first course. Simple, appetizing dish of pasta and oil, Pecorino cheese and black pepper. Tasty and slightly spicy.

Stracciatella: Starter. Light and delicate soup of beaten eggs, cheese and meat broth.

ABRUZZO AND MOLISE

Full-flavored country cooking which is quite spicy as red hot chili peppers are often used. There is not a great variety of dishes to choose from but the flavors of the dishes are very distinctive. The cuisine can be divided into two: the coastal cuisine which is fish-based and the mountain cuisine where the main ingredients include pork, sausages and cheeses. The region's pastries are very good, many contain almonds which are produced in the area.

Cassata all'abruzzese: Dessert. Fine layers of cake soaked in liqueur, alternated with butter cream and pieces of chocolate and *torrone* (See section on "Sweets and Pastries").

Maccheroni alla chitarra: First course. Type of egg pasta with a tomato, onion and bacon sauce or else with *ragù* (See "Basics" section) of lamb. Very apppetizing.

Parrozzo: Dessert. Soft, dry dessert, covered in chocolate.

Scamorza ai ferri: Main course. Typical local cheese which is cut into thin slices and cooked on the grill. Served hot and slightly melted.

Scrippelle: First course. Small omelettes cut into thin strips and served in a meat broth.

REGIONAL DISHES

CAMPANIA

The Campania cuisine is one of the most famous abroad and the place where many of the national dishes originated, such as spaghetti with tomato sauce and pizza. It offers a wide variety of vegetable-based dishes including eggplants, tomatoes and peppers as well as fish and shellfish dishes.

Mozzarella, especially the one made with buffalo's milk, is a basic ingredient of many recipes, while meat is not used that much with the exception of *ragù*. This is a thick tomato sauce in which beef or pork is cooked very slowly (the meat is then removed from the sauce and served separately).

Cecenielli fritti: Starter. Tiny fish which are dipped in batter and then deep-fried.

Gattò di patate: First course. Soft potato cake flavored with pieces of salami and cheese and cooked in the oven.

Impepata di cozze (Mussels): Starter. The mussels are cooked in a pan with oil, garlic and parsley and then served simply in their broth with a generous sprinkling of pepper.

Melanzane ripiene (Stuffed eggplants): Starter. Even if there are several different versions of this recipe, one of the most common is where the eggplant is cut in half and stuffed with a mixture of mozzarella, breadcrumbs, tomatoes and then cooked in the oven.

Pastiera: Rich cake made with puff pastry and filled with ricotta (like cottage cheese made from skimmed milk), wheat and egg which has been lightly flavored with orange.

Sartù di riso: First course. Rice cake flavored with many ingredients including small meatballs, peas, mozzarella cheese, boiled eggs, etc.

Spaghetti alla puttanesca: Pasta/first course. Pasta with a tasty tomato, olive, anchovy and caper sauce.

APULIA

There is a distinctive Mediterranean flavor to the cooking in this region which is based almost exclusively on vegetables, fish, seafood, oil, cheese and pasta. Meat does not appear in many dishes with the exception of lamb. The bread is excellent and has a hard crust.

Carteddate: Dessert. These are sweet strips of fried pastry which are then dipped in honey.

Copete: Dessert. Almond and sugar sweets.

Lampascioni al forno: Starter or side serving. This is a type of bitter-tasting onion which can be found in this region.

Melanzane alla campagnola: Starter or vegetable. Slices of eggplant grilled and seasoned with garlic and various herbs. They are full of flavor and very appetizing.

Minestra di fave (Broad bean soup): First course. Very simple and delicate first course which sometimes has a bitter flavor if *cicoria,* (a bitter-tasting vegetable), is added.

Orata alla barese: Main course. This exquisite and delicately flavored fish is cooked whole in the oven with potatoes, herbs and Pecorino cheese.

Orecchiette alle cime di rapa: Pasta/first course. This pasta, which is often handmade, is seasoned with turnip greens (often used in Apulia) and oil, garlic and red hot chili peppers. Slightly spicy.

Tiella di riso: First course. Rich dish made with rice, mussels, potatoes and sometimes tomatoes.

Tortiera di alici: Starter or main course. Fresh anchovies cooked in the oven with breadcrumbs, herbs and oil.

CALABRIA AND BASILICATA

The cuisine can also be divided in terms of "land" and "sea" in this region too. The meat is almost exclusively pork and lamb, while vegetables include eggplants, peppers, tomatoes. There is a wide variety of fish to choose from in the coastal areas and an ample choice of cold cut meats and cheese is available throughout the regions. Red hot chili peppers are frequently used.

Baccalà alla lucana (Dried salted cod): Main course. The fish is cooked in a pan with pickled peppers. Strong-flavored.

Involtini di pesce spada (Stuffed swordfish rolls): Main course. Slices of the fish are wrapped around a filling of breadcrumbs and herbs and cooked in a pan with white wine.

Macco di fave: First course. Soup made with broad beans and flavored with onions and tomatoes.

Sarde a scapece (sardines): Starter or main course. The fish are fried and seasoned with breadcrumbs and a boiling mix of oil, vinegar and herbs and then left to cool. Strong, aromatic flavor.

Zuppa di pesce di Maratea (Fish soup): First course. The difference between this and similar dishes in other regions is that it is usually flavored with onion and parsley and not tomato and garlic.

SICILY

The Arab influence in this rich cuisine is evident and naturally contains a lot of fish, vegetables and pasta, but not meat. Sicilian cooking often has a bittersweet taste due to the addition of currants and the sauces are generally not as spicy as they are in other southern regions.

Caponata: Starter or main course. Mix of vegetables, mainly eggplants which are cooked in a pan and seasoned with vinegar, capers and raisins.

Cassata: Dessert. Cake filled with a ricotta (like cottage cheese made with skimmed milk), cream and flavored with orange, decorated and has a very sweet flavor.

Cuscus: First course. This dish of Arab origin consists of a type of very fine pasta grain and is usually served with a fish soup or a lamb stew with lots of vegetables.

Farsumagru: Beef stuffed with cold cut meats, egg and cheese and slow-cooked in a tomato sauce.

Gelo di melone: Dessert. This is a type of watermelon jelly which contains little pieces of candied fruit and chocolate. This dessert is also made with other flavors sometimes such as coffee or lemon.

Maccaruni di casa: Pasta. Handmade pasta from flour and water, served with a tomato and meat sauce. Very tasty.

Pasta alla Norma: Pasta/first course. Pasta with tomatoes, fried eggplants and cheese.

Pasta con le sarde (Pasta with sardines): Pasta/first course. Bittersweet flavor, served with fresh fish, raisins and herbs.

Pasta 'ncasciata: Pasta/first course. Pasta with a sauce containing meat, boiled egg and cheese and cooked in the oven.

Pesce al salmoriglio: Main course. The fish is roasted and seasoned with a sauce of oil, lemon, parsley, garlic and oregano.

Pesce spada alla ghiotta (Swordfish): Main course. The fish is cut into slices and cooked with onion, tomato, olives, capers and sometimes raisins.

Sarde a beccafico (sardines): Starter and main course. The fish are stuffed with breadcrumbs and herbs and either fried or cooked in the oven.

Vermicelli alla siracusana: Pasta/first course. Type of spaghetti with tomato, peppers, eggplants, olives and capers.

SARDINIA

One of the most important elements of Sardinian cuisine is the bread which comes in different shapes such as the *carta da musica* (music paper) or the *pane carasau*. Products from the industries of sheep-rearing (lamb and cheese) and fishing, are fundamental, in addition to pasta.

Burrida: Starter. Rich salad of mixed fish with a dressing of oil, vinegar and herbs.

Cordula: Main course. Appetizing dish made from lamb intestines and sometimes served with peas.

Gallina al mirto (Hen): Main course. The bird is boiled and covered in myrtle leaves for 1-2 days. Full flavored and aromatic.

Maccarones con bottarga: Pasta/first course. Handmade pasta with *bottarga* (See section on "Typical products").

Maiale alla brace (Pork cooked on a spit): Main course. The meat is cooked on a spit and covered in herbs. Lamb is also cooked in the same way.

Malloreddus: Pasta/first course. Small, shaped pasta flavored with saffron and a tomato and ricotta (like cottage cheese made with skimmed milk) sauce.

Pane frattau: Starter. This delicate and crunchy local bread is flavored with tomato, egg, oil and cheese.

Pardulas: Dessert. Delicate pastries filled with a fresh cheese cream, flavored with lemon and saffron.

Trattaliu: Main course. Lamb's intestines cooked on a spit or in the oven and flavored with dill.

All recipes serve four portions

INVOLTINI DI CARNE
(Stuffed meat rolls)

Ingredients:

sliced veal or beef	500 g	(1 lb)
sliced raw or cooked ham	100 g	(4 oz)
tin of tomato pulp	200 g	(7 oz)
white wine	half a glass	
butter	40 g	(2 oz)
sage, salt and pepper		

Method:
Remove any fat from the meat and flatten it by beating it lightly. Spread the slices of ham on top of the meat, roll it up, and tie it with a piece of string. Heat the butter in a pan with a few leaves of sage. Add the meat rolls and cook on a high heat for a few minutes until they are cooked on all sides. Add some wine and let it evaporate. Add the tomato, salt and pepper, lower the heat and put the lid on the pan. Simmer for about 45 minutes. Stir occasionally so rolls do not stick to the pan. If the sauce becomes too thick, add some hot water. If towards the end of the cooking time, the sauce becomes too liquid, remove the lid from the pan and increase the heat.

MINESTRONE CON IL RISO
(Soup with rice)

Ingredients:

mixed vegetables of the season	800 g	(approx. 2 lb)
rice	160 g	(5 oz)
small pieces of bacon	40 g	(2 oz)
an onion		
a stock cube		
olive oil, Parmesan cheese		
salt, pepper		

Method:
Chop the bacon and the onion and brown in a pan with 3-4 tablespoons of oil. After a few minutes, add all the vegetables (which have been washed and cut into pieces) and stir in the pan with the bacon and onion for a few minutes. Then add slowly about a liter of boiling water and the stock cube and slowly cook for about 45 minutes (or more if there are beans with the vegetables). Add salt and rice to the soup and cook for another 15 minutes. Remove from the heat for around 15 minutes. Serve with some pepper, grated Parmesan cheese and a little olive oil. For extra flavor, add a tablespoon of *pesto alla genovese* (See "Basics" section) to the soup as soon as it has been removed from the heat.

MOZZARELLA IN CARROZZA

Ingredients:

sliced pan bread	*8 slices*
mozzarella	*4 slices*
eggs	*2*
milk, breadcrumbs, oil	
salt, pepper	

Method:
Remove the crusts from the bread, dip it quickly in a little milk and drain. Make 4 sandwiches with 2 slices of bread and a slice of mozzarella and lightly press them together.
Dip the sandwiches in the beaten eggs, salt and pepper, then in the breadcrumbs making sure that they stick.
Heat around a glassful of oil (preferably sunflower seed oil) in a large pan and fry each of the sandwiches for a few minutes until they are golden brown in color. Serve hot, after they have been placed on a piece of absorbent kitchen paper for a minute.

PARMIGIANA DI MELANZANE
(Eggplants and Parmesan)

Ingredients:

medium-sized eggplants	4	
mozzarella	250 g	(9 oz)
tinned tomato pulp	500 g	(1 lb)
Parmesan cheese	100 g	(4 oz)
eggs	3	
oil, garlic, salt and pepper		

Method:

This dish takes a bit of time to prepare (at least a couple of hours), but is well worth it! Peel the eggplants, slice thinly and lay out in layers on a chopping board, sprinkling a little salt over each layer. Tip the board slightly to one side so that the bitter water coming from the eggplants drains away. After about an hour, rinse the eggplants, dry them and fry them in plenty of sunflower seed oil until they become tender. Remove them from the oil and drain on a piece of absorbent kitchen paper.

Boil the eggs for 10 minutes, peel off the shell and cut into slices. To make the sauce, heat 4-5 tablespoons of olive oil in a pan with a clove of garlic. Remove it when it is golden and add the tomato pulp to the pan. Season it with salt and pepper and cook the sauce on a high heat until it thickens. Add a few leaves (whole) of basil if you have some. In an oven dish, alternate the layers of eggplant, mozzarella and sliced boiled egg, the sauce and grated Parmesan cheese. The last or top layer should be the tomato sauce and Parmesan cheese. Place in the oven at 200 °C (390 °F) for around 20 minutes. Serve hot or warm.

SE RECIPES TO TRY AT HOME

RECIPES TO TRY AT HOME

PASTA AL POMODORO
(Pasta with tomato)

Ingredients:

pasta in a shape of your choice	400 g	(14 oz)
tinned tomato pulp	500 g	(1 lb)
half an onion		
olive oil, Parmesan cheese		
basil, salt, pepper		

Method:
Cut the onion finely and fry over low heat in a pan with 4-5 tablespoons of oil until it becomes golden brown. Add the tomato (better if blended) after a few minutes and a few whole leaves of basil. Cook the sauce over a low heat for about an hour to an hour and a half until it becomes thick. Season it with salt and pepper just before it has finished cooking.
Boil 4 litres (1 gal) of water, add some salt to the boiling water and then the pasta. Cook the pasta, stirring it every once in a while until it is still slightly hard or chewy. Once it has been drained, add the sauce and some grated Parmesan cheese.

PEPERONATA

Ingredients:

red and yellow peppers	600 g	(1⅓ lb)
ripe tomatoes	300 g	(11 oz)
one large onion		
oil, salt, pepper		

Method:
Chop the onion and fry in a pan with 4-5 tablespoons of oil until it turns light brown. Add the peppers which have been cleaned and cut into pieces. Stir the peppers in the oil and onion for a few

68

minutes then add the tomatoes, after they have been peeled, the pulp removed and cut into pieces. Add salt and pepper. Cook together on low heat for about one hour in a covered pan. If the sauce is too liquid after it has finished cooking, remove the lid and increase the heat. If the sauce is too thick, add some hot water.

 ## PIZZA MARGHERITA

Ingredients:

flour	500 g	(1 lb)
yeast for bread	25 g	(1 oz)
tinned tomato pulp	250 g	(9 oz)
mozzarella	150 g	(5 oz)
basil, oil, salt, pepper		

Method:
Melt the yeast in a little warm water and then mix it with a few tablespoons of flour to make a soft dough. Cover the dough with a tea towel and leave it to rise in a warm room until it doubles in volume. Then mix the dough with the remaining flour, 4 tablespoons of oil, a pinch of salt and a glass of warm water. Knead the dough well until it is soft and elastic. If it is too soft, add some flour or add some water if it is too hard. After kneading it by hand for quite a while, shape into a ball and imprint a cross shape on the top. Place it in a bowl covered in flour, cover it with a tea towel and leave it to rise for about an hour in a warm room until it doubles in volume. Then roll the dough with a rolling-pin into a thin disc shape and place it on a large, greased baking tray. Roll up the edges of the dough and season it with tomato, salt and pepper. Cook it in a very hot oven (250 °C, 480 °F) for about 10 minutes, or more if the dough is not very thin. Remove it from the oven and sprinkle it with finely cut pieces of mozzarella, a few basil leaves and a drop of oil, then put it back in the oven until the edges of the dough are golden in color (around 10 minutes).

RECIPES TO TRY AT HOME

 POLLO ALLA CACCIATORA
(Chicken)

Ingredients:

one chicken		
tomato pulp	*200 g*	*(7 oz)*
dried mushrooms	*20 g*	*(1 oz)*
bacon	*70 g*	*(3 oz)*
dry white wine	*half a glass*	
one onion		
half a carrot		
half a stick of celery		
oil, butter, laurel		
salt, pepper		

Method:
Soak the mushrooms in warm water for one hour.
Clean, wash, dry and cut the chicken into 8 pieces. Chop the
bacon, the carrot, onion and celery and brown in a pan with 2
tablespoons of oil and 50 grams (2 oz) of butter. Add the chicken
pieces after a few minutes and brown them slightly over a high
heat. Add the wine and stir until it has evaporated. Lower the
heat, add the tomato, the mushrooms (having drained them first),
a laurel leaf, salt and pepper. Put the lid on the pot and simmer
for about an hour, checking every once in a while that the sauce
does not dry out (if so add some hot water or hot broth.)

 RISOTTO ALLA MILANESE

Ingredients:

rice	*400 g*	*(14 oz)*
meat stock	*1 liter*	*(2 pt)*
butter	*40 g*	*(2 oz)*
one onion		
white wine, saffron		
Parmesan, salt		

70

RECIPES TO TRY AT HOME

Method:
Chop the onion and cook in a pan over a low heat for about 10 minutes, adding a little water if the onion begins to sizzle. Add the rice to the onion and mix well, add a glass of white wine and let it dry, mixing all the time. Start to add some of the meat stock, one cup at a time so that the rice can absorb the liquid before adding more. Stir frequently so that the rice does not stick. Add a packet of saffron to the last cup of broth and add it to the rice. The rice should be cooked after 18 minutes and should appear dry and soft. Remove from the heat, add some salt, a knob of butter and 3-4 tablespoons of grated Parmesan cheese. Mix well and serve.

 SALTIMBOCCA ALLA ROMANA

Ingredients:

sliced veal	500 g	(1 lb)
sliced raw ham	150 g	(5 oz)
flour, sage, white wine		
butter, salt, pepper		

Method:
Remove any excess fat from the meat, beat it lightly until it becomes tender. Cut the meat into pieces which are around the size of the palm of a hand. Sprinkle a little salt over them and dip them in flour, and then shake them to get rid of any excess flour. Place half a slice of ham and a leaf of sage on every piece of meat and attach all of this to the meat with a toothpick.
Heat a large piece of butter in a pan, place the "saltimbocca" in the pan and partly cook on a high heat for a few minutes. When the meat begins to color, add half a glass of white wine and let it dry completely. Serve immediately.

RECIPES TO TRY AT HOME

 ### SPAGHETTI ALLA CHECCA

Ingredients:

large spaghetti	400 g	(14 oz)
large fresh tomatoes	500 g	(1 lb)
basil, olive oil		
Parmesan, salt, pepper		

Method:
Boil plenty of water for the pasta. Dip the tomatoes in the boiling water for a second, remove and then peel them. Cut the tomatoes to remove the pulp from the center and then cut them into small cubes and place in a large bowl. Season them with salt, some chopped basil leaves, 6-7 tablespoons of oil and some pepper. Add some salt to the water as soon as it begins to boil, then the spaghetti and cook until still slightly chewy. Drain the pasta and pour it into the large bowl with the tomatoes. Season with some grated Parmesan cheese and mix well.

 ### SPAGHETTI AGLIO, OLIO E PEPERONCINO

Ingredients:

spaghetti	400 g	(14 oz)
olive oil	half a glass	
garlic, red hot chili peppers		

Method:
Boil around 4 litres (1 gallon) of water; once the water begins to boil add salt and the spaghetti. In the meantime prepare the seasoning: brown two cloves of garlic and one red hot chili pepper in a frying pan. Remove the chili pepper and the garlic once it begins to turn golden in color. Drain the pasta once "al dente" or chewy in texture and slightly hard. Pour the spaghetti into the pan and mix it with the oil over very low heat for one minute. You can garnish it with some chopped parsley.

SPAGHETTI ALLA CARBONARA

Ingredients:

spaghetti	400 g	(14 oz)
smoked bacon	150 g	(5 oz)
Parmesan cheese	100 g	(4 oz)
eggs	3	
olive oil, salt, pepper		

Method:

Boil about 4 litres (1 gallon) of water in a pot and add a large tablespoon of coarse salt, then the pasta and cook over moderate heat for a few minutes, stirring every once in a while.

In the meantime, grate some cheese and mix in with the beaten eggs. Cut the bacon into small pieces and cook it in a frying pan with 4 tablespoons of olive oil until it becomes crunchy.

When the spaghetti is cooked "al dente", that is still slightly hard, drain and pour it back into the pot over very low heat. Pour the beaten egg over the spaghetti and stir quickly so that it becomes creamy. Then add the bacon and oil, stir quickly and remove from the heat. Season with black pepper and serve.

 ## TAGLIATELLE AL RAGÙ

Ingredients:

flour	200 g	(7 oz)
minced meat (beef or veal)	300 g	(11 oz)
sausage	100 g	(4 oz)
tin of tomato pulp	200 g	(7 oz)
eggs	2	
one onion, one carrot		
a stick of celery		
white or red wine		
olive oil, butter, salt, pepper		

Method:
Pour some flour onto a work surface, make a hole in the middle and crack the eggs into the hole. Add a pinch of salt and begin to work the ingredients together first with a knife and then with your hands until you get a smooth hard dough-like mixture. Roll it out with a rolling-pin until it becomes quite thin, sprinkle it with a little flour, roll it up (but not tightly) and then cut it into thin strips. Separate the tagliatelle and leave it to dry for a couple of hours. To make the ragù, chop the onion, carrot and the celery and cook them over low heat in 3 tablespoons of butter and 3 tablespoons of oil for a few minutes. Then add the minced meat and sausage which has been peeled and broken up. Brown the meat and then add half a glass of wine. When the wine has evaporated, add the tomato. Put the lid on the pot and cook slowly for an hour, checking that the sauce does not become too dry. Season with salt and pepper. Boil the tagliatelle for a few minutes in boiling salted water, drain once it is cooked but still slightly hard and add the hot ragù sauce. Garnish with 2-3 tablespoons of grated Parmesan cheese.

 ## TIRAMISÙ

Ingredients:

sugar	150 g	(5 oz)
very soft, sweet, high-fat cheese (such as the Italian mascarpone)	400 g	(14 oz)
dry sponge cake (or soft biscuits)	200 g	(7 oz)
eggs	3	
coffee, rum, cocoa		

Method:
Beat the egg yolks and sugar until creamy, and then add the cheese very slowly and then the tablespoon of rum after that. Whip 1 or 2 egg whites into stiff peaks and then fold them into the cream mixture very carefully.
Soak the biscuits or finely cut sponge cake in the coffee and spread some of it out in a dish. Cover it with half the cream and

then spread the rest of the soaked biscuits or cake. Put the dessert in the refrigerator for a couple of hours and sprinkle some cocoa powder over the top before serving.

VITELLO TONNATO
(Veal and tuna fish)

Ingredients:

a very lean piece of veal	1 kg	(2 lb)
a tin of tuna fish in oil	200 g	(7 oz)
mayonnaise	4 tablespoons	
green olives, capers		
onion, carrot , celery		
salt		

Method:
Tie the piece of meat into the shape of a roast. Boil some water in a pot with a piece of onion, carrot and celery. Then add some salt and place the meat in the pot and boil it for about an hour. Leave the meat to cool in the water, untie it and then cut it into thin slices.
Remove the tuna from its oil and mix it with a spoonful of pitted olives, some capers and 1-2 spoonfuls of the meat broth. Mix it into a smooth cream and add the mayonnaise. Cover the slices of veal with the sauce and serve cold.

ZABAIONE

Ingredients:

egg yolks	4
sugar	4 tablespoons
Marsala wine (or Port or Madiera)	8 tablespoons

Method:
Beat the egg yolks and the sugar until it becomes a clear bubbly mixture. Add the wine, a little at a time while beating the mixture. Put the container in a pot of warm water over a low

heat. Cook the cream and continue to mix, making sure that the water in the pot does not boil. The cream will be ready after about 15 minutes, when it begins to appear quite thick. It can be served hot or cold with cakes, puddings, biscuits or ice-cream.

ZUPPA INGLESE

Ingredients

milk	1 l	(2 pt)
sugar	250 g	(9 oz)
flour	100 g	(4 oz)
cooking chocolate	50 g	(2 oz)
bitter cocoa	25 g	(1 oz)
sugared coffee	one cup	
light biscuits	one packet	
dessert liqueur	half a glass	
egg	one	

Method:
Heat the milk. Beat the eggs with around 120 grams (1 gallon) of sugar and then half the flour: slowly dilute with half of the hot milk and cook the cream over a low heat, mixing all the time until it thickens. Be careful that it does not boil. Leave it to cool, stirring frequently.
Mix the rest of the flour, sugar and cocoa, dilute it in the rest of the milk, adding a little at a time. Make sure that there are no lumps and cook the cream over a low heat, stirring frequently until it thickens. Leave it to cool and mix regularly. When the creams are cool, pour them into a glass dish alternating a layer of dark cream with one of the biscuits which have been soaked in coffee, with one of the yellow colored cream, and then with a layer of the biscuits which have been soaked in liqueur (diluted in some water). Cover the top with a layer of cooking chocolate which has been cut into very fine pieces and keep it in the refrigerator for a few hours before serving.
The liqueur used in Italy for making this dessert is "alchermes", which is red in color and spicy. You can also use rum, orange liqueur or something else.

A di Ancona
a dee an-kohna

B di Bologna
bee dee bol-onya

C di Como
chee dee coh-mo

D di Domodossola
dee dee domo-dos-sola

E di Empoli
ay dee em-polee

F di Firenze
ef-fe dee fee-rent-say

G di Genova
jee dee jenovah

H di Hotel
ak-ka dee oh-tel

I di Imola
ee dee ee-moh-la

J di Jolly
jay dee joh-lee

K di kiwi
kap-pa dee kee-wee

L di Livorno
el-le dee lee-vorno

M di Milano
em-me dee mee-lahno

N di Napoli
en-ne dee nah-polee

O di Otranto
o dee o-tranto

P di Palermo
pee dee palayr-mo

Q di quadro
koo dee kwa-dro

R di Roma
er-re dee roh-ma

S di Savona
es-se dee savoh-na

T di Torino
tee dee toree-no

U di Udine
oo dee oodee-nay

V di Venezia
voo dee vaynayt-see-a

W di whisky
dop-pee-ohvoo dee wees-kee

X *ics*

Y *ipsilon or ee gre-koh*

Z di Zara
dze-ta dee dsara

Things to remember

Bars usually serve bread rolls, croissants or pastries as well as coffee and other drinks. You usually have to pay before ordering and then show your receipt to the barman.

An espresso/ cappuccino	**Un caffè/un cappuccino** *oon ka-fe/oon kap-poot-cheeno*
A draught beer	**Una birra alla spina** *oona beer-ra al-la speena*
A medium sized lager/stout	**Una birra chiara/scura media** *oona beer-ra keyara/skoora med-ee-a*
Two cups of tea with milk	**Due tazze di tè con latte** *doo-ay tat-say dee te kohn lah-tay*
A glass of mineral water	**Un bicchiere d'acqua minerale** *oon beek-ye-ray dakwa meenay-rahlay*
With ice please	**Con ghiaccio, per favore** *kohn gee-at-cho payr fa-vohray*
Another coffee please	**Un altro caffè, per favore** *oon altro kaf-fe payr fa-voh-ray*
Can you bring me the bill please?	**Mi porti il conto, per favore** *mee por-tee eel kohntoh payr fa-vohray*

I have a small baby/
two children

Ho un bambino piccolo/due bambini
*o oon bambeeno peekkolo/doo-ay bam-
beenee*

Do you have a
special rate for
children?

Avete delle riduzioni per bambini?
*a-vaytay dayl-lay reeduts-yohnee payr
bam-beenee*

Have you got a cot
for the baby?

Avete un lettino per il bambino?
*a-vaytay oon layt-teeno payr eel bam-
beeno*

Do you have a
children's menu?

Avete un menu per bambini?
a-vaytay oon maynoo payr bam-beenee

Can you heat the
baby's bottle?

Mi può scaldare il biberon per il bambino?
*mee pwo skal-dahray eel beebay-ron
payr eel bam-beeno*

Where can I
feed/change the
baby?

Dove posso allattare/cambiare il bambino?
*dohvay pos-so al-lat-tahray/kambee-ahray
eel bam-beeno*

Do you have a high
chair?

Avete un seggiolone?
a-vaytay oon say-jaloh-nay

Is there a garden
where the children
can play?

**C'è un giardino dove i bambini possono
andare a giocare?**
*che oon jar-deeno dohvay ee bam-bee-
nee pos-sono an-dahray a jok-ahray*

Can you bring me a
glass of water at
room temperature
please?

**Per favore, mi porti un bicchiere d'acqua
a temperatura ambiente**
*payr fa-vohray, mee por-tee oon beek-ye-
ray dakwa a taympay-ra-toora ambee-
entay*

This doesn't work	**Questo non funziona** _kways_to nohn foonts-_yoh_na
It has a flaw	**È difettoso** _e deefayt-_tohzo_
We are still waiting to be served	**Stiamo ancora aspettando di essere serviti** stee-_ahmo an-_koh_ra aspayt-_tando_ dee es-_sayray sayr-_veetee_
My coffee is cold	**Il caffè è freddo** eel kaf-_fe_ e _frayd_-do
This meat is tough	**Questa carne è dura** _kways_ta _ka_rnay e _doo_ra
My serviette is dirty	**La tovaglia non è pulita** la toh_vah_-leeya nohn e poo-_lee_-ta
The room is noisy	**La stanza è rumorosa** la _stant_sa e roomo-_roh_za
It's too smokey here	**Qui c'è troppo fumo** kwee che _trop_-po _foo_-mo
This wine has not been chilled	**Questo vino non è stato messo in fresco** kw_ays_to _vee_no nohn e _stat_-to _mays_-so een _fresko_

Do you speak English?	**Parla inglese?** _par_la een-_glay_zay
I don't speak Italian	**Non parlo italiano** nohn _par_lo eetal-_yah_no
What's your name? (polite version/ casual version)	**Come si chiama/ti chiami?** _ko_may see kee-_ah_ma/ tee kee-_ah_mee
My name is...	**Mi chiamo...** mee kee-_ah_mo...
Do you mind if I sit here?	**Le dispiace se mi siedo qui?** lay deespee-_a_chay say mee see-_e_-do kwee
Is this place free?	**È libero questo posto?** e _lee_bay-ro kw_ay_sto _po_sto
Where are you from?	**Da dove viene?** da _do_hvay vee-_e_-nay
I'm from...	**Vengo da...** _vayn_-go da...
I'm English/American	**Sono inglese/americano** _soh_noh een-_glay_zay/ahmayree_ca_hno
Can I offer you a coffee/ something to drink?	**Posso offrirle un caffè/qualcosa da bere?** _poh_soh of_freer_-lay oon ka-_fe_/kwal-_ko_za da _bay_ray

First of March
Primo marzo
preemo martso

Second of June
Due giugno
doo-ay joon-yo

We will be arriving
on the 29th of
August
**Arriveremo il 29
agosto**
_arree-vay-raymo
eel vayntee-novay
agos-to_

Nineteen-ninety
seven
**Millenovecentono-
vantasette**
_meel-laynovay-
chento-novahnta-
se-tte_

Monday
lunedì
loonay-dee

Tuesday
martedì
martay-dee

Wednesday
mercoledì
merko-laydee

Thursday
giovedì
jovay-dee

Friday
venerdì
vaynayr-dee

Saturday
sabato
sa-bato

Sunday
domenica
domay-neeka

January
gennaio
jen-na-yo

February
febbraio
fayb-bra-yo

March
marzo
martso

April
aprile
apree-lay

May
maggio
mad-jo

June
giugno
joon-yo

July
luglio
lool-yo

August
agosto
agohs-to

September
settembre
sayt-tem-bray

October
ottobre
ot-toh-bray

November
novembre
novem-bray

December
dicembre
deechem-bray

Excuse me, where is the station?	**Scusi, dov'è la stazione?** *skoo-zee doh-ve la stats-yohnay*
How do I get to the airport?	**Come faccio per andare all'aeroporto?** *kohmay fat-cho payr an-dahray al-la-ayro-porto*
Can you tell me the way to the station?	**Può indicarmi la strada per la stazione?** *pwo eendee-kahrmee la strahda payr la stats-yohnay*
Is this way to the cathedral?	**È questa la strada che va al duomo?** *e kwaysta la strahda kay va al dwomo*
I am looking for the tourist information office	**Sto cercando l'ufficio informazioni turistiche** *sto chayr-kando loof-fee-cho eenfor-mats-yohnee too-reesteekay*
Which road do I take for...?	**Quale strada devo prendere per...?** *kwahlay strahda dayvo prendayray payr...*
How long will it take to get there?	**Quanto tempo ci vuole per arrivarci?** *kwanto tempo chee vwolay payr ar-ree-vahrchee*
Excuse me, can you tell me where the restaurant is...?	**Scusi, mi sa dire dov'è il ristorante...?** *skoo-zee mee sa deeray doh-ve eel ree-sto-rantay...*

Is there a doctor here?	**C'è un dottore qui?** *che oon doht-<u>toh</u>ray kwee*
Call a doctor/an ambulance!	**Chiamate un dottore/un'ambulanza!** *kee-a-<u>mah</u>tay oon doht-<u>toh</u>ray/oon amboo-<u>lant</u>sa*
Get help quickly!	**Andate a chiedere aiuto, presto!** *an-<u>dah</u>tay a kee-<u>e</u>-dayray a-<u>yoo</u>to <u>pre</u>sto*
My wife is about to give birth	**Mia moglie sta per partorire** *<u>mee</u>-a <u>mol</u>-yay sta payr pahrto-<u>ree</u>-ray*
Where's the nearest police station/hospital?	**Dov'è il posto di polizia/l'ospedale più vicino?** *doh<u>ve</u> eel <u>poh</u>stoh dee poleet-<u>see</u>-a/ospay-<u>dah</u>lay pee-<u>oo</u> vee-<u>chee</u>no*
I've lost my credit card/my wallet	**Ho perso la mia carta di credito/il portafoglio** *o perso la <u>mee</u>-a <u>kar</u>ta dee <u>kray</u>-deeto/eel porta-<u>fol</u>-yo*
I've been robbed	**Sono stato derubato** *<u>soh</u>-no <u>stah</u>to day-roo-<u>bah</u>to*
My wallet has been stolen	**Mi hanno rubato il portafoglio** *mee <u>an</u>-no roo-<u>bah</u>to eel porta-<u>fol</u>yo*
My child/handbag is missing	**Ho perso mio figlio/la mia borsa** *o <u>per</u>so <u>mee</u>-o <u>feel</u>-yo/la <u>mee</u>-a <u>bor</u>sa*

Are there any night clubs?	**Ci sono dei locali notturni?** *chee <u>soh</u>noh <u>day</u>-ee lo-<u>kah</u>lee noh-<u>tur</u>nee*
Is there any place/show suitable for children?	**C'è qualche posto/spettacolo adatto ai bambini?** *che kw<u>a</u>l-kay <u>poh</u>sto/spayt-<u>tah</u>kolo ah-<u>daht</u>-to aee bam-<u>bee</u>-nee*
What is there to do in the evenings?	**Cosa si può fare di sera?** *<u>ko</u>za see pw<u>o</u> <u>fah</u>ray dee <u>say</u>ra*
Where is there a cinema/theater?	**Dov'è un cinema/un teatro?** *doh<u>ve</u> oon <u>chee</u>-nayma/oon te-<u>ah</u>-tro*
Can you book the tickets for us?	**Può prenotarci i biglietti?** *pw<u>o</u> prayno-<u>tahr</u>chee ee beel-<u>ye</u>-tee*
Is there a swimming pool?	**C'è una piscina?** *che <u>oo</u>na pee-<u>shee</u>na*
Do you know of any nice excursions to take?	**Ci sono delle belle escursioni da fare?** *chee <u>soh</u>noh <u>day</u>l-lay <u>bel</u>-lay ayskoor-<u>syoh</u>nee da <u>fah</u>ray*
Where can we play tennis/golf?	**Dove possiamo giocare a tennis/a golf?** *<u>doh</u>vay pos-<u>yah</u>mo jo-<u>kah</u>ray a <u>ten</u>nis/a golf*
Is there horseriding/ fishing?	**Si può andare a cavallo/a pescare?** *see pw<u>o</u> an-<u>dah</u>ray a ka<u>val</u>-lo/ a pay-<u>skah</u>ray*

Things to remember

If you want to buy cold cut meats or cheese, the best place to get them is in the salumerie, which are always well supplied. For other purchases (wine, liqueurs, pasta, oil), the prices and quality are excellent in the big supermarkets.

Is this cheese fresh?	**È fresco questo formaggio?** *E fraysco kwaysto formadge-oh?*
Is this an authentic wine?	**È genuino questo vino?** *e gen-weeno kwaysto veeno*
How much does it cost per kilo/per 100 grams?	**Quanto costa al chilo/all'etto?** *kwanto kohsta al keeloh/aletoh*
How long does it stay fresh for?	**Per quanto tempo si conserva?** *payr kwanto tempo see kohnser-vah*
I'll take this/that	**Prendo questo/quello** *prendo kwaysto/kway-lo*
I'd like two bottles of it	**Ne vorrei due bottiglie** *nay vor-re-ee doo-ay bot-teel-eeay*
Can you give me half a kilo of it?	**Me ne dia mezzo chilo** *may nay dee-ah medz-zo keelo*
Can you wrap it up for the journey?	**Può confezionarmelo per il viaggio?** *pwo kohn-faytsee-ohnarmay-lo payr eel vee-adjo*

In Italian, all nouns are either masculine or feminine. Where in English we say "the apple" and "the book", in Italian it is *la mela* and *il libro* because *mela* is feminine and *libro* is masculine. The gender of nouns is shown in the "article" (=words for "the" and "a") used before them:

ARTICLES

Words for "the":

masc. sing.	fem. sing.
il	**la**
l'(+vowel)	**l'**(+vowel)
lo (+z,gn,pn,ps,x,s+consonant)	

masc.plur.	fem. plur.
i	**le**
gli (+vowel,+z,gn,pn, etc.)	

Words for "a":

masculine	feminine
un	**una**
uno (+z,gn,pn,etc)	**un'** (+vowel)

Note: When used after the words a (to, at), da (by, from), su (on), di (of), and in (in, into), the words for "the" contract as follows:

a+il =al	da+il =dal	su+il =sul
a+lo =allo	da+lo =dallo	su+lo =sullo
a+l' =all'	da+l' =dall'	su+l' =sull'
a+la =alla	da+la =dalla	su+la =sulla
a+i =ai	da+i =dai	su+i =sui
a+gli =agli	da+gli =dagli	su+gli =sugli
a+le =alle	da+le =dalle	su+le =sulle

di+il =del	in+il =nel	
di+lo =dello	in+lo =nello	
di+l' =dell'	in+l' =nell'	
di+la =della	in+la =nella	
di+i =dei	in+i =nei	
di+gli=degli	in+gli=negli	e.g. alla casa (to the house)
di+le =delle	in+le =nelle	sul tavolo (on the table)

NOUNS: FORMATION OF PLURALS

For most nouns, the singular ending changes as follows:

masc. sing.	*masc. plur.*	*example*
o	-i	libr<u>o</u> -libr<u>i</u>
e	-i	padr<u>e</u> -padr<u>i</u>
a	-i	artist<u>a</u> -artist<u>i</u>

NOTE: Most nouns ending in -co/-go become -chi/-ghi or -ci/-gi in the plural.

fem. sing.	*fem. plur.*	*example*
a	-e	mel<u>a</u>-mel<u>e</u>
e	-i	madr<u>e</u>-madr<u>i</u>

NOTE: Nouns ending in -ca/-ga become -che/-ghe in the plural; -cia/-gia becomes -ce/-ge or -cie/-gie.

ADJECTIVES

Adjectives normally follow the noun they describe in Italian.
e.g. la mela rossa (the red apple).

Some common exceptions which precede the noun are:
bello *beautiful*, breve *short*, brutto *ugly*, buono *good*, cattivo *bad*, giovane *young*, grande *big*, lungo *long*, nuovo *new*, piccolo *small*, vecchio *old*.

Italian adjectives have to reflect the gender of the noun they describe. To make an adjective feminine, an -a replaces the -o of the masculine.
e.g. rosso - rossa.

Adjectives ending in -e (e.g. giovane) can be either masculine or feminine. The plural forms of the adjective change in the way described for nouns (above).

POSSESSIVE ADJECTIVES

There are two forms in Italian, one "familiar" (tu) and one "formal" (lei) for the 2nd person singular "you." Therefore, for possessive adjectives there are also two forms for "your" singular, as you will note below.

These words also depend on the gender and number of the following noun and not on the sex of the "owner."

	with masc. sing.noun	with fem. sing.noun	with masc. plur.noun	with fem. plur.noun
my	il mio	la mia	i miei	le mie
your (fam./form.)	il tuo/suo	la tua/sua	i tuoi/suoi	le tue/sue
(plural)	il vostro	la vostra	i vostri	le vostre
his/her/its	il suo	la sua	i suoi	le sue
our	il nostro	la nostra	i nostri	le nostre
their	il loro	la loro	i loro	le loro

PRONOUNS

Remember: there are two forms in Italian, one "familiar" (tu) and one "formal" (lei) for the 2nd person singular "you."

SUBJECT

I	io	*ee-o*
you (fam./form.)	tu/lei	*too/lay-ee*
he	lui/egli	*loo-ee/el-yee*
she	lei/ella	*le-ee/el-la*
it (masc.)	esso	*es-so*
(fem.)	essa	*es-sa*
we	noi	*no-ee*
you	voi	*vo-ee*
they	loro	*lohro*
(things: masc.)	essi	*es-see*
(things: fem.)	esse	*es-say*

VERBS

There are three main patterns of endings for verbs in Italian: those ending in -are, -ere and -ire in the dictionary. Two examples of the -ire verbs are shown, since two distinct groups of endings exist. Subject pronouns are shown in brackets because these are often not used. You will note verbs are conjugated differently for "familiar" or "formal" forms.

Present:

	parlare	to speak	**vendere**	to sell
(io)	parlo	I speak	vendo	I sell
(tu/lei)	parli/a	you speak	vendi/e	you sell
(lui/lei)	parla	he/she/it speaks	vende	he/she/it sells
(noi)	parliamo	we speak	vendiamo	we sell
(voi)	parlate	you speak	vendete	you sell
(loro)	parlano	they speak	vendono	they sell

	dormire	to sleep	**finire**	to finish
(io)	dormo	I sleep	finisco	I finish
(tu/lei)	dormi/e	you sleep	finisci/e	you finish
(lui/lei)	dorme	he/she/it sleeps	finisce	he/she/it finishes
(noi)	dormiamo	we sleep	finiamo	we finish
(voi)	dormite	you sleep	finite	you finish
(loro)	dormono	they sleep	finiscono	they finish

Past:

(io)	ho parlato	I spoke	ho venduto	I sold
(tu/lei)	hai/ha parlato	you spoke	hai/ha venduto	you sold
(lui/lei)	ha parlato	he/she/it spoke	ha venduto	he/she/it sold
(noi)	abbiamo parlato	we spoke	abbiamo venduto	we sold
(voi)	avete parlato	you spoke	avete venduto	you sold
(loro)	hanno parlato	they spoke	hanno venduto	they sold

(io)	ho dormito	I slept	ho finito	I finished
(tu/lei)	hai/ha dormito	you slept	hai/ha finito	you finished
(lui/lei)	ha dormito	he/she/it slept	ha finito	he/she/it finished
(noi)	abbiamo dormito	we slept	abbiamo finito	we finished
(voi)	avete dormito	you slept	avete finito	you finished
(loro)	hanno dormito	they slept	hanno finito	they finished

IRREGULAR VERBS

Among the most important *irregular* verbs are the following:

	essere	to be	**avere**	to have
(io)	sono	I am	ho	I have
(tu/lei)	sei/è	you are	hai/ha	you have
(lui/lei)	è	he/she/it is	ha	he/she/it has
(noi)	siamo	we are	abbiamo	we have
(voi)	siete	you are	avete	you have
(loro)	sono	they are	hanno	they have

	andare	to go	**fare**	to do
(io)	vado	I go	faccio	I do
(tu/lei)	vai/va	you go	fai/fa	you do
(lui/lei)	va	he/she/it goes	fa	he/she/it does
(noi)	andiamo	we go	facciamo	we do
(voi)	andate	you go	fate	you do
(loro)	vanno	they go	fanno	they do

GREETINGS

Hello	**Buongiorno** *bwon jorno*
Good evening	**Buonasera** *bwona sayra*
Good night	**Buonanotte** *bwona not-tay*
Goodbye	**Arrivederci** *ar-reevay-dayrchee*
See you soon	**A presto!** *a presto*
How do you do?	**Piacere!** *pee-a-chayray*
How are you?	**Come sta?** *kohmay sta*
Fine, thank you	**Bene, grazie** *benay grats-yay*
Please	**Per favore** *payr fa-vohray*
Excuse me	**Mi scusi** *mee skoo-zee*
I'm sorry	**Mi dispiace** *mee deespee-achay*
(Many) thanks	**(Molte) grazie** *moltay grats-yay*
Yes please/no thanks	**Sì grazie/no grazie** *see grats-yay/ noh grats-yay*
I would like/we would like..	**Vorrei/vorremmo...** *vor-re-ee/vor-ray-mmo*

I'd like to book a single/double room	**Vorrei prenotare una stanza singola/ doppia** *vorre-ee prayno-tahr-ray oona stantsa seengola/dop-ya*
I'd like a room and breakfast/half board/full board	**Vorrei una camera con prima colazione/ mezza-pensione/pensione completa** *vorre-ee oona ka-mayra kohn preema kolats-yohnay/ medz-za paynsee-ohnay/paynsee-ohnay kompleta*
How much does it cost per day/per week?	**Quanto costa al giorno/alla settimana?** *kwanto costa al jorno/ alla sayt-tee-mahna*
Does the price include breakfast?	**La colazione è compresa nel prezzo?** *la kolats-yohnay e kom-prayza nayl pretso*
We will be staying for three nights from... until...	**Ci fermiamo per tre notti dal... fino al...** *chee fayr-meeahmo per tray not-tee dal... feeno al...*
We will arrive at...	**Arriveremo alle...** *ahree-vay-raym-mo allay...*

Things to remember

If you want to explore the Italian restaurants and trattorie, it is better to book your hotel at half board only.

We booked the room in the name of...	**Abbiamo prenotato una stanza a nome di...** *abbee-<u>ah</u>mo prayno-<u>tah</u>to <u>oo</u>na st<u>a</u>nza a <u>noh</u>may dee...*
Can you have my bags brought up to the room?	**Può far portare su il mio bagaglio?** *pw<u>o</u> fahr por-<u>tah</u>ray soo eel <u>mee</u>-o bagal-yeeo*
What time is breakfast/lunch/dinner at?	**A che ora è la colazione/ il pranzo/la cena?** *a kay <u>oh</u>ra e la kolats-<u>yoh</u>nay/eel pr<u>a</u>ntso/la ch<u>a</u>yna*
Can we have breakfast in our room at...?	**Possiamo avere la colazione in camera alle...?** *pos-<u>yah</u>-mo a-<u>vay</u>ray la kolats-<u>yoh</u>nay een k<u>a</u>mayra <u>a</u>llay...*
Can I have my key?	**Posso avere la mia chiave?** *p<u>o</u>s-so a-<u>vay</u>ray la <u>mee</u>-a kee-<u>ah</u>vay*
Put it on my bill	**Lo metta sul mio conto** *lo m<u>ay</u>t-ta sool <u>mee</u>-o <u>koh</u>ntoh*
I'd like an outside line please	**Mi dà la linea, per favore?** *mee dah la <u>lee</u>nay-a payr fa-<u>voh</u>ray*
May I have another cover/another pillow?	**Posso avere un'altra coperta/un altro cuscino?** *p<u>o</u>s-so a-<u>vay</u>ray oon<u>al</u>-tra ko-<u>payr</u>ta/ oon altro coo-<u>shee</u>-noh*
I have locked myself out of my room	**Sono rimasto chiuso fuori dalla mia stanza** *<u>soh</u>noh ree-<u>mas</u>to kee-<u>oo</u>zo <u>fwo</u>ree <u>day</u>-la <u>mee</u>-a st<u>a</u>ntsa*

A pint of...	**Un mezzo litro di...** *oon medz-zo leetro dee...*
A liter of...	**Un litro di...** *oon leetro dee...*
A kilo of...	**Un chilo di...** *oon keelo dee...*
A pound of...	**Un mezzo chilo di...** *oon medz-zo keelo dee...*
100 grammes of...	**Un etto di...** *oon et-to dee...*
A slice of...	**Una fetta di...** *oona fayt-ta dee...*
A portion of...	**Una porzione di...** *oona portsee-ohnay dee...*
A dozen...	**Una dozzina di...** *oona dodz-zeena dee...*
Two thousand lira's worth of...	**Duemila lire di...** *dooaymeelah leeray dee...*

Things to remember

The bank note with the highest denomination is the 100.000 lira bill. The other notes include 50.000, 10.000, 5.000, 2.000 and 1.000 lire. Coins are available in 500, 200, 100 and 50. Coins of a lower value than these are worth little or nothing.

I haven't enough money

Non ho abbastanza soldi
nohn o ab-ba-stantsa soldee

Have you any change?

Avete da cambiare?
a-vaytay da kambee-ahray

Can you change a fifty thousand lire note?

Può cambiarmi un biglietto da centomila lire?
pwo kambee-ahrmee oon beel-yayt-to da chen-to meela leeray

I would like to change some pounds/dollars into lire

Vorrei cambiare queste sterline/dollari in lire
vor-re-ee kambee-ahray kwaystay stayr-leenay/dol-lahree een leeray

What is the rate for dollars?

Qual è il cambio per i dollari?
kwahle eel kamb-yo payr ee dol-lahree

0	**zero**	13	**tredici**	50	**cinquanta**
	dzero		*tray-deechee*		*cheenkwanta*
1	**uno**	14	**quattordici**	60	**sessanta**
	oono		*kwat-tordeechee*		*says-santa*
2	**due**	15	**quindici**	70	**settanta**
	dooay		*kween-deechee*		*sayt-tanta*
3	**tre**	16	**sedici**	80	**ottanta**
	tray		*say-deechee*		*oht-tanta*
4	**quattro**	17	**diciassette**	90	**novanta**
	kwat-tro		*deechas-set-tay*		*noh-vanta*
5	**cinque**	18	**diciotto**	100	**cento**
	cheen-kway		*deechot-to*		*chento*
6	**sei**	19	**diciannove**	101	**centouno**
	se-ee		*deechan-novay*		*chento-oonoh*
7	**sette**	20	**venti**	110	**centodieci**
	set-tay		*vayntee*		*chento-dee-echee*
8	**otto**	21	**ventuno**	200	**duecento**
	ot-to		*vayn-toono*		*doo-ay-chento*
9	**nove**	22	**ventidue**	300	**trecento**
	novay		*vayntee-doo-ay*		*tray-chento*
10	**dieci**	23	**ventitre**	1000	**mille**
	dee-e-chee		*vayntee-tray*		*meel-ay*
11	**undici**	30	**trenta**	2000	**duemila**
	oondeechee		*trayn-ta*		*doo-ay-meela*
12	**dodici**	40	**quaranta**	1000000	**un milione**
	dohdeechee		*kwaran-ta*		*oon meel-yohnay*

1st	**primo**	5th	**quinto**	9th	**nono**
	preemo		*kweento*		*nonoh*
2nd	**secondo**	6th	**sesto**	10th	**decimo**
	saykohn-do		*sesto*		*dechee-mo*
3rd	**terzo**	7th	**settimo**		
	tayrtso		*set-teemo*		
4th	**quarto**	8th	**ottavo**		
	kwarto		*oht-tahvo*		

Things to remember

Cake shops make and sell a wide range of high quality cakes
and pastries. It is definitely worth trying some.

What are these/those?	**Cosa sono questi/quelli?** _ko_za _sohn_oh kwaystee/kwayllee
What's in this cake?	**Cosa c'è in questa torta?** _ko_za che een _kway_sta _tor_ta
I would like a small/medium sized tray of pastries	**Vorrei un vassoio piccolo/medio di paste** vor-_re_-ee oon vas-_so_-yo _peek_-kolo/_med_-yo dee _pas_tay
I would like an assortment of pastries	**Vorrei delle paste assortite** vor-_re_-ee _dell_-ay _pas_tay as-sohr-_teet_-ay
I'll have a cone for 2000 lire with vanilla and chocolate ice-cream with/without cream	**Prendo un cono da 2000 lire, alla crema e cioccolata con/senza panna** _prayn_-doh oon _kohn_oh da _doo_-ay _meel_-ah _lee_ray alla _cray_ma e chok-ko-_lah_ta kohn/_sen_tsa _pan_na
I'd like an ice-cream in a cup worth 2000 lire	**Vorrei un gelato in coppetta da 2000 lire** vor-_re_-ee oon jay-_lah_to een kop-_pay_tta da doo-ay _meel_a _lee_ray
How much does it/do they cost?	**Quanto costa/costano?** _kwan_to _koh_sta/_koh_stano
Is there chocolate in those cakes?	**C'è del cioccolato in quelle paste?** che del chok-ko-_lah_to een _kway_llay _pas_tay

How much is it?	**Quanto costa?** *kwanto kohsta*
Can I have the bill please?	**Mi può portare il conto, per favore?** *mee pwo por-tahray eel kohntoh payr fa-vohray*
Can I pay by credit card?	**Posso pagare con carta di credito?** *pos-so pa-gahray kohn karta dee kray-deeto*
Do you accept cheques/traveller's cheques?	**Accettate assegni/traveller's check?** *at-chayt-tahtay as-saynyee/traveller's cheques*
Can I have the receipt please?	**Mi dà la ricevuta, per favore?** *mee dah la reechay-voota payr fa-vohray*
Is service/tax included?	**Il servizio è compreso/l'IVA è compresa?** *eel sayrveets-yo/leeva e kom-prayza*
What does that come to?	**Quanto fa in tutto?** *kwanto fa een toot-to*
Do I pay in advance?	**Devo pagare in anticipo?** *dayvo pa-gahray een antee-cheepo*
Do I have to leave a deposit?	**Devo lasciare un acconto?** *dayvo lashahray oon ak-kohnto*
I think you have given me the wrong change	**Mi sembra che mi abbia dato il resto sbagliato** *mee saym-bra kay mee abee-ya dah-to eel raysto sbal-yahto*

Do you make pizzas at lunch?	**Fate pizze anche a pranzo?** *fah-tay pizz-ay ahn-kay ah pran-tso?*
What type of starters do you have?	**Che antipasti avete?** *kay antee-pahs-tee ah-vay-tay?*
What is on this pizza?	**Che ingredienti ci sono in questa pizza?** *kay een-gray-dee-en-tee chee so-no in kwesta pizza?*
A "margherita" without mozzarella	**Una "margherita" senza mozzarella** *oona "mar-gayr-ee-ta" sen-tsa mo-tsar-rel-la*
I'll have this one but without onion/salame/anchovies	**Va bene questa ma senza cipolle/salame/acciughe** *va bay-nay kweysta ma sen-tsa chee-pol-lay/sal-la-may/a-choo-gay*
Can you substitute the... with...?	**Può sostituire il... con... ?** *pwo sos-tee-tooee-ray eel... cohn...*
I'd like it very thin/thick	**La vorrei molto sottile/bella alta** *la vor-re-ee molto so-tee-lay/bella ahl-ta*
I'd like only a little oil	**Mi raccomando, poco olio** *mee rak-ko-mahn-do po-co oh-lyo*
A cold/room temperature Coke/fruit juice	**Una Coca/un succo di frutta freddo/a temperatura ambiente** *oona coca/oon sook-ko dee froot-ta/ah tem-per-ah-tur-ah ahm-bee-en-tay*

Can you help me please?	**Può aiutarmi, per favore?** *pwo a-yoo-tahr mee payr fa-vohray*
What is the matter?	**Che cosa c'è** *kay koza che*
What's happening?	**Che cosa succede?** *kay koza soot-che-day*
I need help	**Ho bisogno di aiuto** *o beezohn-yo dee a-yooto*
I don't understand	**Non capisco** *nohn ka-peesko*
Do you speak English?	**Parla inglese?** *parla een-glayzay*
Can you repeat that please?	**Può ripetere, per favore?** *pwo re-pe-tayray payr fa-vohray*
I have run out of money	**Sono rimasto senza soldi** *sohnoh ree-masto sentsa soldee*
My son/daughter is lost	**Non trovo più mio figlio/mia figlia** *nohn trohvoh pee-oo mee-o feel-yo/mee-a feel-ya*
I have lost my way	**Mi sono perso** *mee sohnoh payrso*
Leave me alone!	**Lasciami in pace!** *lash-amee een pa-chay*

In the pronunciation system used in this book, Italian sounds are
represented by spellings of the nearest possible sounds in English.
Hence, when you read out the pronunciation – the line in *italics*
after each phrase or word – sound the letters as if you were reading
an English word. Whenever we think it is not sufficiently clear
where to stress a word or phrase, we have used underlined *italics* to
highlight the syllable to be stressed. The following notes should help
you:

	REMARKS	EXAMPLE	PRONUNCIATION
ay:	As in *day*	meno	*may-nnoh*
ah:	As in *father*	prendiamo	*prend-yahmo*
e:	As in *bed*	letto	*let-to*
oh:	As in *go*	sono	*sohnoh*
y:	As in *yet*	aiuto	*a-yooto*
ow:	As in *cow*	auto	*owto*

Spelling in Italian is very regular and, with a little practice, Italian
words can be pronounced from their spelling alone. The only letters
which may cause problems are:

i	As *ee* in *meet*	vino	*veeno*
	or as *y* in *yet*	aiuto	*a-yooto*
u	As *oo* in *boot*	luna	*loona*
	or as *w* in *will*	buon	*bwon*
c	Before e,i as *ch* in *chat*	centro	*chentro*
	Before a,o,u as in *cat*	cosa	*koza*
ch	As *c* in *cat*	chi	*kee*
g	Before e,i as in *gin*	giorno	*jorno*
	Before a,h,o,u as in *get*	regalo	*ray-gahlo*
gl	As *lli* in *million*	figlio	*feel-yo*
gn	As *ni* in *onion*	bisogno	*beezohn-yo*
h	Silent	ho	*o*
sc	Before e,i, as *sh* in *shop*	uscita	*oo-sheeta*
	Before a,o,u, as in *scar*	capisco	*ka-peesko*
z	As *ts* in *cats*	senza	*sentsa*
	or *ds* in *rods*	mezzo	*medz-zo*

New Year's Day	**Capodanno**
Epiphany	**Epifania**
Easter	**Pasqua**
Easter Monday	**Lunedì dell'Angelo**
Liberation Day	**Liberazione (April 25)**
Assumption Day	**Assunzione (ferragosto, August 15)**
Labor Day	**Festa del lavoro (May 1)**
All Saints' Day	**Ognissanti (November 1)**
Immaculate Conception	**Immacolata (December 8)**
Christmas	**Natale**
St. Stephen's Day	**Santo Stefano (December 26)**

Is it far?	**È lontano?** *e lon-tahno*
Is it expensive?	**Costa molto?** *kohsta mol-toh*
Did you understand?	**Ha capito?** *a kap-ee-to*
Can you help me?	**Può aiutarmi?** *pwo a-yoo-tahrmee*
Where are the shops?	**Dove sono i negozi?** *dohve sohnoh ee naygots-ee*
How do I get there?	**Come ci si arriva?** *kohmay chee see ar-reeva*
What is this?	**Che cos'è questo?** *kay koz-ay kwaysto*

Good evening, we'd like a table for two

Buonasera, vorremmo un tavolo per due
bwona-sayra, vor-raym-mo oon tah-volo payr doo-ay

We'd like a table in a quiet corner

Vorremmo un tavolo in un angolo tranquillo
vor-raym-mo oon tah-volo een oon an-golo trankweel-lo

We booked a table for 2 in the name of...

Abbiamo prenotato un tavolo per 2, a nome...
ab-beeam-mo pray-nohtahto oon tah-volo payr doo-ay, a noh-may...

Can we eat outside?

Si può mangiare all'aperto?
see pwo man-jahray al-a-perto

We'd like a table far from/near the window

Vorremmo un tavolo lontano dalla/vicino alla finestra
vor-raym-mo oon tah-volo lon-tahno dah-la/vee-cheeno ahl-la fee-nestra

Is there a wheelchair entrance?

C'è un'entrata per disabili?
che oon ayn-trahta payr dees-abeelee

Do you speak English?

Parla inglese?
parla een-glayzay

Do you have a fixed-price menu?

Avete un menu a prezzo fisso?
ahvay-tay oon maynoo a prets-so feesso

I/we would like...

Vorrei/vorremmo...
vor-re-ee/vor-raym-mo

Waiter!	**Cameriere!** *kamay-ree-<u>ay</u>ray*
Is there a long wait?	**C'è molto da aspettare?** *ch<u>e</u> <u>mol</u>to da ah-spay-<u>tar</u>-ray?*
Where is the cloak room?	**Dov'è il guardaroba?** *doh-<u>ve</u> il gwarda-<u>ro</u>ba?*
Is there a coat hook?	**C'è un attaccapanni?** *ch<u>e</u> un ah-tahka-<u>pan</u>-nee?*
Can you turn on the fan?	**Può azionare il ventilatore?** *pw<u>o</u> ah-zee-oh-<u>nar</u>-ray il ven-tee-la-<u>tor</u>-ray?*
Can you bring me some bread sticks, please?	**Può portare dei grissini, per favore?** *pwo por-<u>tah</u>ray d<u>a</u>yee gree-<u>see</u>nee payr fa-<u>voh</u>ray?*
What drinks do you have?	**Che bibite avete?** *kay <u>bee</u>-beetay ah-<u>vay</u>tay?*
What brands of beer do you have?	**Che marche di birra avete?** *kay <u>mahr</u>-kay di b<u>ee</u>r-rah ah-<u>vay</u>tay?*
A quarter liter of house wine, please	**Un quartino di sfuso, per favore** *oon kwar<u>teen</u>-oh di s<u>foo</u>so, payr fa-<u>voh</u>ray*
Where is the starter table?	**Dov'è il tavolo degli antipasti?** *doh-<u>vay</u> il <u>tah</u>-vohlo d<u>a</u>ylee ahn-tee-<u>pah</u>stee?*
Is the fish fresh or frozen?	**Il pesce è fresco o congelato?** *il <u>pay</u>-shay ay <u>fres</u>-ko oh cohn-djel-<u>ah</u>-toe?*
Does this come with a side dish?	**Questo piatto comprende anche un contorno?** *kw<u>a</u>ysto pee-<u>ah</u>-toe cohm-<u>pren</u>-day <u>ahn</u>-kay oon cohn-<u>tor</u>no?*

Can I have mixed side dishes?	**Si possono avere contorni misti?** *si <u>pos</u>-so-no ah-<u>vay</u>-ray cohn-<u>tor</u>-nee <u>mees</u>-tee?*
I'd like it cooked with little salt	**Lo vorrei cucinato con poco sale** *lo vor-<u>re</u>-ee ku-chee-<u>nah</u>-toe cohn <u>po</u>-co <u>sah</u>-le*
I'd like the meat rare/medium/well-done	**Vorrei la carne al sangue/poco cotta/ben cotta** *vor-<u>re</u>-ee la <u>kar</u>-nay al <u>sang</u>-way/<u>po</u>-co <u>koh</u>-tta/ben <u>koh</u>tt-ta*
Can you heat this please?	**Me la fa riscaldare, per piacere?** *may la fah rees-kal-<u>dar</u>-ray, payr pee-a-<u>chay</u>-ray*
I did not order this dish	**Non ho ordinato questo piatto** *non o or-deen-<u>ah</u>-toe <u>kway</u>sto pee-<u>aht</u>-toe*
Please pass me the salt/oil	**Mi passa il sale/l'olio, per cortesia?** *mee <u>pas</u>-sa il <u>sah</u>-le/l'<u>oh</u>-<u>lee</u>-o, payr kor-teh-<u>zee</u>-a?*
Do you have ice-cream?	**Avete gelati?** *ah-<u>vay</u>-tay jay-<u>lah</u>-tee?*
I'd like a dry/sweet sparkling wine	**Vorrei uno spumante dolce/secco** *vor-<u>re</u>-ee <u>oo</u>no spoo-<u>mahn</u>-tay <u>dol</u>-che/<u>say</u>-ko*
A digestive, thank you	**Un digestivo, grazie** *oon dee-djes-<u>tee</u>-vo, <u>grats</u>-yay*
I think there is an error in the bill	**Credo che ci sia un errore nel conto** *<u>kray</u>-do kay chee <u>see</u>-a oon ayr-<u>ro</u>-ray nel <u>cohn</u>-to*

Can we see the menu?	**Possiamo vedere il menu?** *possee-ahmo vay-dayray eel maynoo*
Do you have a vegetarian menu?	**Avete un menu vegetariano?** *a-vaytay oon maynoo vayjay-tar-yahno*
What is the house specialty?	**Qual è la specialità della casa?** *kwahle la spaycha-leeta day-la kasa*
What is the dish of the day?	**Qual è il piatto del giorno?** *kwahle eel peeat-to dayl jorno*
What do you recommend?	**Che cosa ci consiglia?** *kay kosa chee konseel-ya*
What's in this dish?	**Cosa c'è in questo piatto?** *kosa che een kwaysto peeat-to*
Is it spicy?	**È piccante?** *e peek-kantay*
I'm allergic to peppers	**Sono allergico al peperone** *sohnoh al-layr-jeeko al paypay-rohnay*
Is there garlic/pepper in this dish?	**Questo piatto contiene dell'aglio/del pepe?** *kwaysto peeat-to kohn-tee-enay dayl al-yo/ dayl paypay*
Do you have...?	**Avete...?** *a-vaytay*
Can you bring me the bill please?	**Mi porti il conto, per favore** *mee por-tee eel kohntoh payr fa-vohray*

Can you bring me/us...?	**Mi/ci porti...** *mee/chee por-tee...*
I would like a portion/half a portion of...	**Vorrei una porzione/mezza porzione di...** *vor-re-ee oona ports-yohnay/medz-za ports-yohnay dee*
I'd like to taste...	**Vorrei assaggiare...** *vor-re-ee as-sad-jaray...*
Can you bring us some more bread please?	**Ci porti dell'altro pane, per favore** *chee por-tee dayl altro panay payr fa-vohray*
What are the typical dishes of the area?	**Quali sono i piatti tipici della zona?** *kwahlee sohnoh ee peeat-ee tee-peechee daylla zona*
What is the typical cheese of the area?	**Qual è il formaggio tipico della zona?** *kwahle eel formad-jo tee-peeko daylla zona*
What desserts/fruit do you have?	**Che dolci/frutta avete?** *kay dolchee/froot-ta a-vaytay*
We'd like a portion of... with two plates	**Vorremmo una porzione di... con due piatti** *vor-raym-mo oona ports-yohnay dee... kohn doo-ay peeatee*
Can you bring me salt/pepper?	**Mi porta il sale/il pepe?** *mee portah eel sahlay/eel paypay*
Four cups of coffee please	**Quattro caffè, per favore** *kwat-tro kaf-fe payr fa-vohray*
Can we see the wine list?	**Possiamo vedere la lista dei vini?** *pos-seeahmo vay-dayray la leesta day-ee veeni*

Can I book a table for four please?	**È possibile prenotare un tavolo per quattro, per favore?** *e pos-see-beelay prayno-tahray oon tah-volo payr kwat-tro payr fa-vohray*
I'd like to book a table for two people for this evening/tomorrow evening at eight, in the name of...	**Vorrei prenotare un tavolo per due persone, per questa sera/domani sera alle otto, a nome...** *vor-re-ee prayno-tahray oon tah-volo payr doo-ay payr-sohnay, payr kwaysta say-rah/do-mahnee say-rah al-lay ot-to, a noh-may...*
Which day is it closed during the week?	**Qual è il giorno di chiusura settimanale?** *kwahle eel jorno dee keeoo-zoo-ra sayt-teema-nahlay*
What time does the restaurant open/close?	**A che ora apre/chiude il ristorante?** *a kay ohra ah-pray/keeoo-day eel reesto-rantay*
I'd like to cancel a booking I made for this evening, for 2 people in the name of...	**Vorrei disdire una prenotazione che avevo fatto per questa sera, per 2 perso-ne, a nome...** *vor-re-ee dees-dee-ray oona prayno-tats-yohnay kay avayvo fat-to payr kwaysta sayra, payr doo-ay payr-sohnay, a noh-may...*
Is it necessary to book?	**È necessario prenotare?** *e naychays-saryo pray-nohtaray*

We'd like an aperitif	**Vorremmo un aperitivo** *vor-raym-mo oon a-payree-teevo*
What wine would you recommend with this dish?	**Che vino ci consiglia con questo piatto?** *kay veeno chee konseel-ya kohn kwaysto peeat-to*
Can you recommend a good white/red/rosé wine?	**Ci può consigliare un buon vino bianco/ rosso/rosato?** *chee pwo konseel-yahray oon bwon veeno bee-anko/ros-so/ro-zahto*
Can you bring us the house wine please?	**Ci porti il vino della casa, per favore** *chee por-tee eel veeno daylla kasa payr fa-vohray*
A/half bottle of...	**Una/mezza bottiglia di...** *oona/medz-za bot-teelya dee...*
A bottle of natural/sparkling mineral water please	**Per favore, una bottiglia d'acqua minerale naturale/gassata** *payr fa-vohray oona bot-teelya dakwa meenay-rahlay natoorahlay/gas-sata*
Can you bring us another bottle of water/wine please?	**Per favore, ci porti un'altra bottiglia d'acqua/di vino** *Payr fa-vohray, chee portee oon-altra bot-teel-ya dakwa/dee veeno*
What are the typical wines/liqueurs of the area?	**Quali sono i vini/i liquori tipici della zona?** *kwahlee sohnoh ee veenee/ ee lee-kwoh-ree tee-peechee daylla dzo-nah*
What bitters/liqueurs do you have?	**Che amari/liquori avete?** *kay a-mahree/lee-kwohree a-vaytay*

Things to remember

> So-called ristoranti are not the only places where you can eat.
> There are also pizzerie, trattorie, spaghetterie and osterie.

Is there a good restaurant in this area?	**C'è un buon ristorante in questa zona?** *che oon bwon reesto-rantay een kwaysta dzo-nah*
Is there a cheap restaurant near here?	**C'è un ristorante economico qui vicino?** *che oon reesto-rantay ayko-no-meeko kwee vee-cheeno*
Do you know of a restaurant with traditional cooking?	**Mi può indicare un ristorante con cucina tipica?** *mee pwo een-deekaray oon reesto-rantay kohn koo-cheena tee-peeka*
How do I get there?	**Come ci si arriva?** *kohmay chee see ar-reeva*
Excuse me, can you tell me where the restaurant...is?	**Scusi, mi sa indicare dov'è il ristorante...?** *skoo-zee, mee sa een-deekaray doh-ve eel reesto-rantay...*
What is the best restaurant in the city?	**Qual è il migliore ristorante della città?** *kwahle eel meel-yohray reesto-rantay dayl-la cheet-ta*
We want to find a cheap restaurant for lunch	**Vorremmo pranzare in un ristorante poco costoso** *vor-raym-mo prant-sahray een oon reesto-rantay poko koh-stohzoh*

Excuse me, where is the toilet?	**Scusi, dov'è la toilette?** *skoo-zee, doh-ve la twalet*
Is there a telephone here?	**C'è un telefono, qui?** *che oon tayle-fono kwee*
Can I have an ashtray?	**Posso avere un portacenere?** *posso a-vayray oon porta-chay-nayray*
Can you bring me another glass/plate?	**Mi può portare un altro bicchiere/piatto?** *mee pwo por-tahray oon-altro beek-ye-ray/peeat-to*
Can you change my fork/knife/spoon please?	**Mi cambia la forchetta/il coltello/il cucchiaio, per favore?** *mee kambya la forkayt-ta/eel koltel-lo/eel kook-ya-yo payr fa-vohray*
Can you lower/raise the heating?	**Si può abbassare/alzare il riscaldamento?** *see pwo ab-bahs-saray/al-tsaray eel ree-skal-da-maynto*
Can you open/close the window?	**Si può aprire/chiudere la finestra?** *see pwo a-preeray/keeoo-dayray la fee-nestra*
I've got a stain, have you got talcum powder?	**Mi sono macchiato, avete del borotalco?** *mee sohnoh mak-keeyah-to, a-vaytay dayl boro-talko*
What time do you close?	**A che ora chiudete?** *a kay ohra kee-oodaytay*
Can you call a taxi for us?	**Ci può chiamare un taxi, per favore?** *chee pwo keea-mahray oon taksee payr fa-vohray*

Things to remember

In Italy, it is forbidden to smoke in public places, (museums, cinemas etc.) and on the public transport (subway, bus). There are designated carriages for smoking on trains.

Can I smoke here?
Si può fumare qui?
see pwo foo-mahray kwee

Do you mind if
I smoke?
Le dispiace se fumo?
lay deespee-achay say foomo

May I have an
ashtray?
Posso avere un portacenere?
pos-so a-vayray oon porta-chay-nayray

Do you have
matches?
Avete dei fiammiferi?
a-vaytay day-ee fee-am-mee-fayree

Have you got a
light?
Ha da accendere?
a da at-chen-dayray

Do you mind
putting out that
cigarette?
Le dispiace smettere di fumare?
lay deespee-achay smayt-tayray dee foo-mahray

Things to remember

There are authorized taxi companies. The cars are usually yellow or white. Do not trust the "private" taxis or, if you do use one, agree on a price before getting into the taxi.

Can you call me a taxi please?	**Può chiamarmi un taxi, per favore?** *pwo kee-a-<u>mahr</u>mee oon <u>taxsee</u> payr fa-<u>voh</u>ray*
To the main station/ to the airport	**Alla stazione centrale/all'aeroporto** *<u>al</u>-la stats-<u>yoh</u>nay chayn-<u>trah</u>lay/allaer-oh-<u>por</u>to*
Take me to this address/this hotel	**Mi porti a questo indirizzo/a questo albergo** *mee <u>por</u>tee a <u>kway</u>sto een-dee<u>reets</u>-so/<u>kway</u>sto al-<u>bayr</u>go*
Is it far?	**È lontano?** *e lon-<u>tah</u>no*
I'm in a hurry	**Ho molta fretta** *o <u>moh</u>lta <u>fray</u>-ta*
How much will it cost?	**Quanto verrà a costare?** *<u>kwan</u>to ver-<u>ra</u> a ko-<u>stah</u>ray*
Please stop here/at the corner	**Si fermi qui/all'angolo** *see <u>fayr</u>mee kwee/al-<u>lan</u>-golo payr fa-<u>voh</u>ray*
How much is it?	**Quant'è?** *kwan<u>te</u>*
Can you give me a receipt?	**Può farmi una ricevuta?** *pwo <u>fahr</u>mee <u>oo</u>na reechay-<u>voo</u>ta*

Things to remember

> Many public telephones take coins (100, 200 o 500 lire), but
> card phones are also quite widespread. Telephone cards can be
> bought at the tobacconist's, newspaper kiosks or special auto-
> matic vending machines.

I'd like an outside line	**Mi dà la linea?** *mee dah la leenay-a*
Can I have a telephone card for 5.000/10.000 lire?	**Mi dà una scheda telefonica da 5.000/10.000 lire?** *mee dah oona skaydah taylay-fon-eeka da cheen-kway/dee-e-chee meela leeray*
I'd like to make a phone call	**Vorrei fare una telefonata** *vor-re-ee fahray oona taylay-fo-nahta*
The number is... extension...	**Il numero è..., interno...** *eel noo-mayro e... een-tayrno...*
How much is it to phone England?	**Quanto costa telefonare in Inghilterra?** *kwanto kohsta taylay-fo-nahray een een-geel-ter-ra*
I can't get through	**Non riesco a prendere la linea** *nohn ree-esko a pren-dayray la leenay-a*
What's the prefix for...?	**Qual è il prefisso per...** *kwahl-e eel pray-fees-so payr...*
Can you give me change in 200/500 lire coins?	**Può cambiarmeli in monete da 200/500 lire?** *pwo kamb-yahr-may-ly een mo-naytay da doo-ay chento/cheen-kway chento leeray*
The line's busy	**La linea è occupata** *la leenay-a e ok-koo-pahta*

Hello, this is...

Pronto, sono...
prohntoh <u>soh</u>noh...

Can I speak to...?

Posso parlare con...?
<u>pos</u>-so par-<u>lah</u>ray kohn...

I've been cut off

Mi è stata tolta la comunicazione
mee e <u>stah</u>ta <u>tol</u>ta la kom-moonee-kats-<u>yoh</u>nay

I'm sorry, wrong number

Scusi, ho sbagliato numero
<u>skoo</u>-zee o zbal-<u>yah</u>to <u>noo</u>-mayro

It's a bad line

Non si sente bene
nohn see <u>say</u>ntay <u>be</u>nay

YOU MAY HEAR: ────────────

Pronto, chi parla?
<u>prohn</u>toh kee <u>par</u>la

Hello who's speaking?

Resti in linea
<u>ray</u>stee een <u>lee</u>nay-a

Hold the line

Riprovi più tardi, per favore
ree-<u>proh</u>vee pee-<u>oo</u> <u>tar</u>dee payr fa-<u>voh</u>ray

Please try again later

Non c'è
nohn che

He/she is not here

Ha sbagliato numero
a zbal-<u>yah</u>to <u>noo</u>-mayro

You have got the wrong number

What time is it?	**Che ore sono?** *kay ohray sohnoh*
It's...	**Sono le...** *sohnoh lay...*
8:00	**le otto** *lay ot-to*
8:05	**le otto e cinque** *lay ot-to ay cheen-kway*
8:10	**le otto e dieci** *lay ot-to ay dee-echee*
8:15	**le otto e un quarto** *lay ot-to ay oon kwarto*
8:20	**le otto e venti** *lay ot-to ay vayntee*
8:30	**le otto e mezza** *lay ot-to ay medz-za*
8:40	**le nove meno venti** *lay novay mayno vayntee*
8:45	**le nove meno un quarto** *lay novay mayno oon kwarto*
8:50	**le nove meno dieci** *lay novay mayno dee-e-chee*
Eight A.M./P.M.	**Le otto del mattino/della sera** *lay ot-to dayl mat-teeno/daylla sayra*
Midday	**Mezzogiorno** *medz-zo-jorno*
Midnight	**Mezzanotte** *medz-za-nottay*

What time do you open/close?	**A che ora apre/chiude?** *a kay ohra apray/kee-ooday*
What time does the restaurant close?	**A che ora chiude il ristorante?** *a kay ohra kee-ooday eel reesto-rantay*
What time do the shops close?	**A che ora chiudono i negozi?** *a kay ohra kee-oodono ee naygots-ee*
How long will it take to get there?	**Quanto ci vorrà per arrivarci?** *kwanto chee vor-ra payr ar-ree-vahrchee*
We arrived early/late	**Siamo arrivati presto/tardi** *see-ahmo ar-reevahtee presto/tardee*
It's early/late	**È presto/tardi** *e presto/tardee*
What time does the coach leave?	**A che ora parte l'autobus?** *a kay ohra partay lowto-boos*
The table is booked for... this evening	**Il tavolo è riservato per le... di questa sera** *eel tah-volo e reezayr-vahto payr lay... dee kwaysta sayra*

| Where are the toilets please? | **Dov'è la toilette, per favore?** |
| | *doh<u>ve</u> la twa<u>let</u> payr fa<u>voh</u>ray* |

Do you have to pay for the toilets?

La toilette è a pagamento?
la twa<u>let</u> e a paga-<u>mayn</u>to

There's no toilet paper/soap

Non c'è carta igienica/sapone
nohn che <u>kah</u>rta ee-<u>je</u>-neeka/sa-<u>poh</u>nay

Is there a toilet for the disabled?

C'è una toilette per disabili?
che <u>oo</u>na twa<u>let</u> payr dis-<u>a</u>beelee

The toilet is blocked

Il W.C. è otturato
eel voo chee e ot-too<u>ra</u>-to

GASTRONOMIC
DICTIONARY

ITALIAN-ENGLISH

abbacchio *m* lamb
abbacchio a scottadito: see section on "Regional Dishes", p. 57
abbacchio brodettato: see section on "Regional Dishes", p. 57
abbastanza enough
abbrustolito toasted
accanto nearby; **accanto a** beside
accendere to light; to turn on
acceso(a) lit; on
acciuga *f* anchovy
acerbo sour; bitter
aceto *m* vinegar
aceto balsamico *m* balsamic vinegar; see section on "Other Specialties", p. 25
acido acid; sour
acqua *f* water **acqua gassata** *f* sparkling water **acqua minerale** *f* mineral water **acqua naturale** *f* still water
acquacotta: see section on "Regional Dishes", p. 55
acquavite *f* brandy
addebitare to debit; to charge
additivo *m* additive
adulto *m* adult
aereo *m* aeroplane
aeroporto *m* airport
affettati misti *m pl* selection of cold cut meats; see section on "National Dishes", p. 33
affettato sliced (also for cold cuts)
affogato: see section on "National Dishes", p. 33
affollato crowded
affumicato smoked
Aglianico del Vulture: see section on "Wines", p. 16

aglio *m* garlic
agnello *m* lamb
agnello arrosto see section on "National Dishes", p. 33
agnolini: see section on "Pasta", p. 14
agnolotti: see section on "Pasta", p. 14
agosto *m* August
agro sour; bitter
agrodolce: all'agrodolce: bittersweet see section on "Gastronomic Terms", p. 29
agrume *m* citrus fruit
aiutare to help
Albana: see section on "Wines", p. 16
albergo *m* hotel
albicocca *f* apricot
albume *m* egg white
Alcamo: see section on "Wines", p. 16
alcolici *mpl* alcoholic drinks
alcolico alcoholic
alcuni some; a few (pl.)
Aleatico: see section on "Wines", p. 16
alimentazione *f* nourishment; feeding
allergia *f* allergy
allevamento *m* upbringing (children); breeding (animals)
alloro *m* bay leaf
almeno at least
altro other
amarena *f* sour cherry
amaretti: see section on "Sweets and Pastries", p. 23
amaretto *m* bitter liqueur
Amaretto di Saronno: see section on "Liqueurs", p. 21
amaro (as a noun/adjective) bitter

Amarone: see section on "Wines", p. 16

amatriciana, pasta alla: see section on "National Dishes", p. 33

ambasciata *f* embassy

amico(a) *m/f* friend

amido *m* starch

analcolico non-alcoholic

ananas *m* pineapple

anatra *f* duck

anche also; too; as well

ancora still; yet

andare to go

angolo *m* angle; corner

anguilla *f* eel

anguilla arrosto (or **alla griglia**) *f* roasted or grilled eel; see section on "National Dishes", p. 33

anguilla in umido *f* eel in tomato sauce; see section on "National Dishes", p. 34

anguria *f* watermelon

anice *f* anise

animelle *fpl* sweetbread

annata *f* year (ref. to wine)

anno *m* year

anolini: see section on "Pasta", p. 14

antibiotico *m* antibiotic

antipasto *m* appetizer; hors d'oeuvre

antipasto di verdure: see section on "Regional Dishes", p. 48

aperitivo *m* aperitif

aperto/all'aperto open; on/ open air

apparecchiare to set the table

appetito /buon appetito *m* appetite/ enjoy your meal

appuntamento *m* appointment/ date

apribottiglie *m* bottle-opener

aprile *m* April

apriscatole *m* tin-opener

arachide *f* peanut

aragosta *f* spiny lobster; crayfish

arancia *f* orange

aranciata *f* orangeade

arancini di riso: see section on "National Dishes", p. 34

aria/aria condizionata *f* air/ air conditioning

aringa *f* herring

arista: see section on "Regional Dishes", p. 55

aroma/ aromi *f* aroma /fragrances

aromatico aromatic; spiced

arrabbiata: all'arrabbiata: see section on "Gastronomic Terms", p. 29; **penne alla:** see section on "National Dishes", p. 34

arrivare to arrive

arrostito roasted; toasted

arrosto *m* roast; see section on "National Dishes", p. 34

arrosto in crosta *m* roast meat in pastry; see section on "National Dishes", p. 34

arrosto misto di pesce/pesce arrosto *m* mix of baked fish/baked fish; see section on "National Dishes", p. 34

ascensore *m* lift; elevator

asciugamano *m* towel

asiago: see section on "Cheeses", p. 8

asparagi *mpl* asparagus

asparagi alla Bismark: see section on "National Dishes", p. 34 ; **involtini di asparagi:** see section on "National Dishes", p. 34

aspettare to wait
aspirina f aspirin
assaggiare to taste
assaggio m taste
assegno m check
Asti spumante: see section on "Wines", p. 16
astice m lobster
attendere to wait
attento attentive; alert; be careful
Aurum: see section on "Liqueurs", p. 21
Austria Austria
austriaco Austrian
autentico authentic; genuine; original
autobus m bus
avanti forward; ahead; on
avena f oats
avere to have
avocado m avocado
avvertire to point out; to notify; to inform; to warn

babà: see section on "National Dishes", p. 35
bacca f berry
baccalà alla lucana: see section on "Regional Dishes", p. 62
baccalà fritto f fried fish; see section on "National Dishes", p. 35
baccalà mantecato: see section on "Regional Dishes", p. 51
bagna caoda: see section on "Regional Dishes", p. 48
bagno m bath; swim
ballare to dance
bambino(a) m/f child
banana f banana
banca f bank

bar m bar
barbabietola f beet
Barbaresco: see section on "Wines", p. 16
Barbera: see section on "Wines", p. 16
Bardolino: see section on "Wines", p. 16
barista m barman
Barolo: see section on "Wines", p. 16
basilico m basil
bastare to be sufficient; to be enough
bavarese Bavarian: see section on "National Dishes", p. 35
bavette: see section on "Pasta", p. 14
bellavista: in bellavista: see section on "Gastronomic terms", p. 29
bello(a) beautiful; lovely
bene well; good
benvenuto welcome
bere to drink
besciamella f bechamel; see section on "Basics", p. 27
bevanda f drink
bianco white **in bianco** without tomatoes
Bianco di Pitigliano: see section on "Wines", p. 17
bibita f drink
bicchiere / bicchierino m glass/liqueur glass
biete o bietole f chard or beetgreens
biglietto m ticket
bignè m cream puff
bigoli: see section on "Pasta", p. 14
bigoli in salsa: see section on

"Regional Dishes", p. 51

birra *f* beer **chiara/scura/alla spina/piccola/ grande** lager/stout/draught/small/ large

biscotto *m* biscuit

bisogno *m* need **avere bisogno di** to have need of

bistecca *f* steak **ai ferri** steak grilled

bistecca alla fiorentina *f* steak cooked Florentine style; see section on "National Dishes", p. 35

bocca *f* mouth

bocconcini: *mpl* titbit; morsel: see section on "Gastronomic Terms", p. 29

bollente boiling

bollire to boil

bollito boiled (also for meat)

bollito con salsa pearà: see section on "Regional Dishes", p. 51

bollito misto *m* mixture of boiled meat; see section on "National Dishes", p. 35

bolognese: alla bolognese: see section on "Gastronomic Terms", p. 29

bomba di riso: see section on "Regional Dishes", p. 54

bombolone *m* doughnut

bombolotti: see section on "Pasta", p. 14

bonet: see section on "Regional Dishes", p. 48

borotalco *m* talcum powder

borsa *f* bag

borsetta *f* handbag

boscaiola: alla boscaiola: see section on "Gastronomic Terms", p. 29

boscaiola, pasta alla: see section on "National Dishes", p. 35

bottarga: see section on "Other Specialties", p. 25

bottiglia *f* bottle

bottone *m* button

bovino *m* bovine

brace: alla brace: see section on "Gastronomic Terms", p. 29

braciola *f* chop (meat)

branzino *m* bass

brasato braised

brasato al Barolo *m*: see section on "Regional Dishes", p. 48

brasato al vino *m* braised beef cooked in wine; see section on "National Dishes", p. 35

bresaola: see section on "Cold Cut Meats", p. 11 and "National Dishes", p. 35; **involtini di:** see section on "National Dishes", p. 36

brindisi *m* toast

brocca *f* jug

broccoli *mpl* broccoli

broccoli, pasta e: see section on "National Dishes", p. 36

brodetto: see section on "Regional Dishes", p. 56

brodetto [di pesce] *m* fish soup; see section on "National Dishes", p. 36

brodo *m* broth/ soup

bruciare to burn

bruciato(a) burnt

Brunello di Montalcino: see section on "Wines", p. 17

bruschetta: see section on "National Dishes", p. 36

brutto(a) bad; ugly

bucatini: see section on "Pasta", p. 14

budino *m* pudding
bue *m* ox
buongustaia: alla buongustaia: see section on "Gastronomic Terms", p. 29
buono(a) good
burrata: see section on "Cheeses", p. 8
burrida: see section on "Regional Dishes", p. 64
burro *m* butter
busecca: see section on "Regional Dishes", p. 50
busta *f* envelope; packet

Cabernet: see section on "Wines", p. 17
cacao *m* cocoa
cacciagione *f* game (animal)
cacciatora: alla cacciatora: see section on "Gastronomic Terms", p. 29
cacciatorini: see section on "Cold Cut Meats", p. 11
cacciucco: see section on "Regional Dishes", p. 55
cachi *m* khaki
cacio *m* cheese
caciocavallo: see section on "Cheeses", p. 8
caciotta: see section on "Cheeses", p. 8
cadere to fall
caffè *m* coffee **lungo/espresso/macchiato/decaffeinato** weak black coffee/strong short coffee/coffee with a dash of milk/ decaffeinated
calamari *mpl* squid
calamari ripieni/imbottiti *mpl* stuffed squid; see section on "National Dishes", p. 36

caldo(a) hot
calmante calming; sedative
calmo(a) calm
calorie *fpl* calories
calzagatti: see section on "Regional Dishes", p. 54
calzoni: see section on "National Dishes", p. 36
cambiare to change
cambio *m* change; exchange
camera *f* room
cameriera or **cameriere** *f/m* maid /waiter
camicia *f* shirt
camminare to walk
camomilla *f* camomile
campagna *f* countryside; campaign
cancellare to cancel
candela *f* candle
canditi *mpl* candied
canederli: see section on "Regional Dishes", p. 52
canestrato: see section on "Cheeses", p. 8
cannella *f* cinnamon; tap
cannelloni: see section on "Pasta", p. 14 and "National Dishes", p. 36
cannoli: see section on "Sweets and Pastries", p. 23
cannolicchi: see section on "Pasta", p. 14
Cannonau: see section on "Wines", p. 17
canocchia *f* squill
cantina *f* cellar; wine shop
canzone *f* song
capellini: see section on "Pasta", p. 14
capesante o cappesante medium-sized white fleshed

scallop (Coquille St Jacques)
capire to understand
capocollo: see section on "Cold Cut Meats", p. 11
Capodanno *m* New Year's Day
capogruppo *m* group-leader
capolinea *m* end of the line
caponata: see section on "Regional Dishes", p. 62
cappelletti/tortellini/agnolini in brodo: see section on "National Dishes", p. 37
cappello *m* hat
capperi *mpl* capers
cappon magro: see section on "Regional Dishes", p. 49
cappone *m* capon
cappotto *m* (over)coat
caprese: see section on "National Dishes", p. 37
capretto *m* kid (gloves)
capretto al forno *m* roast kid; see section on "National Dishes", p. 37
Capri: see section on "Wines", p. 17
caraffa *f* carafe; decanter
caramella *f* sweet; candy
caramello *m* caramel
carbonara, pasta alla: see section on "National Dishes", p. 37
carciofo *m* artichoke
carciofi alla giudia: see section on "Regional Dishes", p. 57
carciofi alla romana: see section on "Regional Dishes", p. 58
cardi *mpl* cardoons
carne *f* meat **macinata o tritata** pounded or minced
carne all'albese: see section on "Regional Dishes", p. 48

carne in scatola tinned meat
caro(a) dear; expensive
carota *f* carrot
carpaccio: see section on "National Dishes", p. 37
carpione di pesce *m* marinated fish; see section on "National Dishes", p. 37
carré square (sliced bread)
carrello *m* shopping trolley; shopping cart (USA)
carrettiera: alla carrettiera: see section on "Gastronomic Terms", p. 30
carrozzina *f* pram; push-chair
carta paper **alla carta** à la carte
carta di credito *f* credit card
carta di identità *f* identity card
carteddate: see section on "Regional Dishes", p. 61
cartoccio: al cartoccio: see section on "Gastronomic Terms", p. 30
cartoccio, pasta al: see section on "National Dishes", p. 37
cartolina *f* postcard
casa/della casa: see section on "Gastronomic Terms", p. 30
casalinga: alla casalinga: see section on "Gastronomic Terms", p. 30
cassa *f* box; cash desk; check-out
cassata: see section on "Regional Dishes", p. 63
cassata all'abruzzese: see section on "Regional Dishes", p. 59
casseruola: in casseruola: see section on "Gastronomic Terms", p. 30
cassiera *f* cashier
cassoeula: see section on "Regional Dishes", p. 50

castagna f chestnut

castagnaccio: see section on "Regional Dishes", p. 55

Castel del Monte: see section on "Wines", p. 17

Castelli Romani: see section on "Wines", p. 17

castelmagno: see section on "Cheeses", p. 9

castrato m mutton; lamb

cattivo(a) bad; evil

cavatelli (or **cavatieddi**): see section on "Pasta", p. 14

caviale m caviar

cavolfiore m cauliflower

cavolini di Bruxelles mpl Brussels sprouts

cavolo m cabbage

cecenielli fritti: see section on "Regional Dishes", p. 60

ceci mpl chick-peas

ceci, pasta e: see section on "National Dishes", p. 38

cedro m citron

CEE f EEC (European Economic Community)

cefalo m gray mullet

cena f supper; dinner

cenere f ash(es)

Centerbe: see section on "Liqueurs", p. 21

cento hundred

centrale central

centro m center

cereali mpl cereals

cernia f grouper

cerotto m plaster; Band Aid (USA)

cervella or **cervello** m/f brains

cetriolini mpl gherkin

cetriolo m cucumber

champagne f champagne

che who; which; that; what

chi who; which

chiamare to call

chiamata /al telefono telephone call/ on the telephone

Chianti: see section on "Wines", p. 17

chiaro(a) clear; pale

chiedere to ask

chiodini mpl honey mushrooms

chiudere to close

chiuso(a) closed

chiusura f closure

cialzons: see section on "Regional Dishes", p. 53

ciambella f ring-shaped cake; bun

ciaramicola: see section on "Regional Dishes", p. 57

ciccioli: see section on "Other Specialties", p. 25

cicoria f chicory

ciliegia f cherry

cima alla genovese: see section on "Regional Dishes", p. 49

Cinque Terre: see section on "Wines", p. 17

cioccolata f chocolate

cioccolatini mpl chocolates

cioccolato m chocolate

cipolla f onion

Cirò: see section on "Wines", p. 17

città f city

ciuccio m baby's pacifer

cliente m/f client; customer

cocco m coconut

cocomero m watermelon

coda alla vaccinara f oxtail; see section on "National Dishes", p. 58

cognome m surname; last name (USA)

colazione f breakfast; lunch
Colli Albani: see section on "Wines", p. 17
Colli Berici: see section on "Wines", p. 17
Colli Euganei: see section on "Wines", p. 18
Colli Lanuvini: see section on "Wines", p. 18
Colli del Trasimeno: see section on "Wines", p. 18
Collio: see section on "Wines", p. 18
coloranti mpl coloring; food dyes
colore m color
coltello m knife
come like; as; such as; how; why
cominciare to start
comitiva f party; group; company
comodo convenient; comfortable
comprare to buy
compreso included
comunicazione f announcement; message; communication
con with
conchiglia f shell
conchiglie: see section on "Pasta", p. 14
conchiglioni: see section on "Pasta", p. 14
condimento m flavoring; seasoning; dressing
confermare to confirm
confetti mpl sugar-coated almonds; see section on "Sweets and Pastries", p. 23
confettura f jam; marmalade
confezionato(a) ready-made; ready-to-wear
congelato(a) frozen
coniglio m rabbit
coniglio alla cacciatora m rabbit cacciatore; see section on "National Dishes", p. 38
coniglio alle olive m rabbit with olives; see section on "National Dishes", p. 38
cono m cone
conservanti mpl preservatives
conservato(a) preserved; kept
contadina: alla contadina: see section on "Gastronomic Terms", p. 30
contante cash **in contanti** in cash
contento(a) happy
continuare to continue
conto m bill; account
contorno m vegetables
contro against
controllare to control; to check
coperto m place; cover; charge **al coperto** indoors
copete: see section on "Regional Dishes", p. 61
coppa or **coppetta** f bowl; cup
coppa: see section on "Cold Cut Meats", p. 11
coprire to cover
cordula: see section on "Regional Dishes", p. 64
cornetto m roll; croissant
corposo(a) full-bodied
corrente f power (electricity); current
cosa f thing; **che cosa?** what?
coscia: coscia di pollo f chicken leg
costare to cost
costata f entrecote

costine *fpl* ribs (of a leaf)
costo *m* cost
costoletta *f* cutlet
costolette/cotolette alla bolognese *m* cutlets/chops cooked Bolognese style; see section on "National Dishes", p. 38
costolette/cotolette alla milanese *m* cutlets/chops cooked Milanese style; see section on "National Dishes", p. 38
costoso(a) expensive
cotechino: see section on "Cold Cut Meats", p. 12
cotechino in camicia: see section on "Regional Dishes", p. 54
cotoletta *f* cutlet; see section on "The Basics", p. 27
cotone *m* cotton
cotto(a) cooked
cottura *f* cooking; baking
cozze *fpl* mussels
cozze alla marinara/sauté di cozze *fpl* sautéed mussels; see section on "National Dishes", p. 38
cravatta *f* tie
crema: see section on "The Basics", p. 27 **alla crema:** *f* cream; see section on "Gastronomic Terms", p. 30
crema fritta *f* fried cream; see section on "National Dishes", p. 38
crespelle *f* fried pastry twist
croccante *f* crisp
crocchette *fpl* croquettes
crosta/in crosta: see section on "Gastronomic Terms", p. 30

crostacei *mpl* shellfish
crostata *f* jam tart
crostata alla ricotta: ; see section on "National Dishes", p. 38
crostata di frutta: see section on "National Dishes", p. 39
crostini *mpl* croutons; canapé; see section on "National Dishes", p. 39
crostini di milza: see section on "Regional Dishes", p. 55
crostino: see section on "Regional Dishes", p. 58
crostino al prosciutto: see section on "Regional Dishes", p. 58
crudità *fpl* raw vegetables
crudo(a) raw; uncooked
cubetto: cubetto di ghiaccio *m* cube/ice-cube
cucchiaio *m* spoon **cucchiaino** teaspoon
cucina *f* kitchen
culatello: see section on "Cold Cut Meats", p. 12
cumino *m* cumin; cummin
cuocere to cook
cuoco(a) cook
cuscino *m* cushion; pillow
cuscus: see section on "Regional Dishes", p. 63
custode *m/f* caretaker; keeper
custodire to keep; to guard

dado *m* bouillon cube
dare to give
datteri *mpl* dates (fruit)
davanti in front; opposite
debole weak

decorato(a) decorated
decorazione *f* decoration
dente: al dente: see section on "Gastronomic Terms", p. 30
dentice *m* dentex
dentiera *f* denture; set of false teeth
dentro in; inside
depositare to settle (wine); to deposit
dessert *m* dessert
destra right **a destra** on the right
diabetico(a) diabetic
diavola: alla diavola: see section on "Gastronomic Terms", p. 31
dicembre *m* December
dieta *f* diet
dietro behind; after
difficile difficult
digeribile digestible
digestivo *m* digestive
dimenticare to forget
dintorni *mpl* surroundings
dire to say
direttore *m* director
direzione *f* management; direction
diritto *m* right; right side
disabile disabled
discoteca *f* discothèque; disco
disdire to cancel
disinfettante *m* disinfectant
disinfettare to disinfect
distanza *f* distance
distributore *m* distributor
disturbare to disturb
ditali: see section on "Pasta", p. 14
diverso(a) different
documenti *mpl* papers (passport)
dolce [noun/adj.] *m* sweet; dessert; cake
Dolcetto: see section on

"Wines", p. 18
dolcificante *m* sweetener
dolciumi *mpl* sweets
dollari *mpl* dollars
domanda *f* question; demand; application (job)
domani tomorrow
domenica *f* Sunday
donna *f* woman
dopo after; afterward(s)
doppio(a) double
dorato(a) browned; golden brown
dove where
dovere to have to; must
duro(a) hard; tough; harsh

economico(a) economical; inexpensive; cheap
elenco/elenco telefonico *m* list/telephone directory
eliche: see section on "Pasta", p. 14
entrare to enter
entrata *f* entrance
Erbaluce di Caluso: see section on "Wines", p. 18
erbazzone: see section on "Regional Dishes", p. 54
erbe aromatiche *fpl* herbs
errore *m* error; mistake
escursione *f* excursion
esperto(a) expert; experienced
espresso *m* express letter; express train; coffee
Est!Est!!Est!!!: see section on "Wines", p. 18
estate *f* summer
esterno(a) outside; external
estivo(a) summer; summery
estratto *m* extract
etichetta *f* etiquette; tag; label

evitare to avoid

facile easy
fagiano *m* pheasant
fagioli *mpl* beans
fagioli al fiasco: see section on "Regional Dishes", p. 55
fagioli all'uccelletto: see section on "Regional Dishes", p. 55
fagioli con le cotiche *mpl* beans with pig rind; see section on "National Dishes", p. 39
fagioli, pasta e: see section on "National Dishes", p. 39
fagiolini *mpl* green beans
fagottini: see section on "Gastronomic Terms", p. 31
Falerio: see section on "Wines", p. 18
fame *f* hunger
famiglia *f* family
familiare family; familiar
famoso(a) famous
faraona *f* guinea fowl
farcito(a) stuffed
fare to do; to make
farfalle: see section on "Pasta", p. 14
farina *f* flour
farinata: see section on "Regional Dishes", p. 49
farmacia *f* chemist's shop
farsumagru: see section on "Regional Dishes", p. 63
fattura *f* invoice
fave *fpl* broad beans
favore *m* favor **per favore** please
fazzoletto di carta *m* tissue (handkerchief)
febbraio *m* February
fegato/fegatini *m/mpl* liver/livers

fegato alla veneta *m* liver cooked veneto style; see section on "National Dishes", p. 39
feriale weekday
ferie *fpl* holidays
fermare to stop; to close
fermata *f* stop **del bus / della metro** bus stop/metro stop
ferri: ai ferri: see section on "Gastronomic Terms", p. 31
fesa *f* rump
festa *f* party; holiday
fetta *f* slice
fettina *f* slice (of meat)
fettuccine: see section on "Pasta", p. 14
fettuccine ai piselli: see section on "National Dishes", p. 39
fiamma, alla *f* flame; flambé
fiammifero *m* match
fiasco *m* straw-covered flask
fichi in crocetta: see section on "Sweets and Pastries", p. 23
fico *m* fig
figlio/figlia *m/f* son/daughter
filetti *mpl* fillets
filetto *m* fillet
filetto al pepe verde *m* fillet with green pepper; see section on "National Dishes", p. 39
filo *m* thread; grain; wire
filtrare to filter
fine *f* end; conclusion; purpose
finestra *f* window
finferli *mpl* mountain mushrooms
finire to finish
fino a until; as far as
finocchio *m* fennel
finocchiona: see section on "Cold Cut Meats", p. 12
fiocchetto: see section on "Cold

Cut Meats", p. 12
fiocchi *mpl* flakes
fior di latte: see section on "Gastronomic Terms", p. 31
fiore *m* flower
fiore sardo: see section on "Cheeses", p. 9
fiori di zucca fritti *mpl* fried zucchini flowers; see section on "National Dishes", p. 39
Firenze Florence
firma *f* signature
focaccia *f* (flat) cake; bun; see section on "Other Specialties", p. 25
fonduta: see section on "National Dishes", p. 39
fontina: see section on "Cheeses", p. 9
forchetta *f* fork
formaggio *m* cheese
forno *m* oven
forse perhaps
forte strong; loud
fotografia *f* photograph
fra between; among(st)
fragola *f* strawberry
fragole con panna *fpl* strawberries with cream; see section on "National Dishes", p. 40
francese French
Francia France
francobollo *m* stamp
frappé *m* ice-cream and milk-shake
Frascati: see section on "Wines", p. 18
frattaglie *mpl* offal; giblets
freddo(a) cold
fresco(a) cool; fresh; wet (paint)
fretta: avere fretta/ fare in fretta hurry: to be in a hurry/ to do

something in a hurry
frico: see section on "Regional Dishes", p. 53
frigorifero *m* refrigerator
frittata *f* omelette
frittelle *fpl* frittèrs
fritto(a) fried fritto misto [di pesce] mixed fry (of fish); see section on "National Dishes", p. 40
frittura *f* frying; fry
frizzante fizzy; sparkling
frolla, pasta *f* short pastry
frollini biscuits
frullare to beat; to whip up; to whisk
frullato *m* fruit and milk-shake
frutta *f* fruit frutta fresca/frutta secca fresh fruit/ dried fruit
frutti di bosco fruits of the forest
frutti di mare seafood
frutti di marzapane/di Martorana: see section on "Sweets and Pastries", p. 23
fumante smoking; steaming
fumare to smoke
fumatore *m* smoker
funghi *mpl* mushrooms
funghi freschi /funghi secchi fresh mushrooms/ dried mushrooms
funghi, pasta ai *mpl* pasta with mushrooms; see section on "National Dishes", p. 40
funzionare to work (mechanism)
fuoco *m* fire
fuori outside; out (not at home)
fusilli: see section on "Pasta", p. 14

gabinetto *m* toilet
galletto *m* cockerel; young cock
gallina *f* hen

gallina al mirto: see section on "Regional Dishes", p. 64

gallinaccio *m* mountain mushrooms

gamba *f* leg

gamberetti/gamberi *mpl* shrimps, prawns /crayfish

garofalato di bue: see section on "Regional Dishes", p. 58

gassato(a) gassed; fizzy

Gattinara: see section on "Wines", p. 18

gattò di patate: see section on "Regional Dishes", p. 60

gelateria *f* ice-cream shop

gelatina *f* jelly

gelato *m* ice-cream; see section on "Sweets and Pastries", p. 23

gelo di melone: see section on "Regional Dishes", p. 63

genere *m* kind (type); gender

generi alimentari *mpl* foodstuffs

genitori *mpl* parents

gennaio *m* January

Genova Genoa

germogli *mpl* buds; sprouts

gettare to throw

ghiaccio *m* ice

ghiacciolo *m* ice lolly

giacca *f* jacket

giallo(a) yellow

gianduiotti: see section on "Sweets and Pastries", p. 24

giardino *m* garden

ginepro *m* juniper

giocare to play

giornale *m* newspaper

giornata *f* day

giorno *m* day

giovane young; young person

giovedì *m* Thursday

girare to turn; to spin

giro *m* tour; turn

gita *f* trip; excursion

giù down; downstairs

giugno *m* June

glassa *f* icing

gnocchetti: see section on "Pasta", p. 14

gnocchi alla bava: see section on "National Dishes", p. 40

gnocchi alla romana: see section on "National Dishes", p. 40

gnocchi di patata: see section on "Other Specialties", p. 25

gnocco fritto: see section on "Regional Dishes", p. 54

gola *f* throat

gorgonzola: see section on "Cheeses", p. 9

gradire to accept; to like

Gran Bretagna Great Britain

grana padano: see section on "Cheeses", p. 9

granchio *m* crab

grande big; great; large

granita *f* water ice; see section on "Sweets and Pastries", p. 24

grano *m* grain

granturco *m* maize

Grappa: see section on "Liqueurs", p. 21

grasso(a) fat

gratin: al gratin: see section on "Gastronomic Terms", p. 31

gratinato(a) sprinkled with cheese and breadcrumbs and browned in the oven

grattugiato(a) grated

gratuito(a) free

grazie thank you

greco(a) Greek

Greco di Tufo: see section on "Wines", p. 18

griglia f grill: **alla griglia:** see section on "Gastronomic Terms", p. 31

Grignolino: see section on "Wines", p. 18

grissini mpl bread-sticks; see section on "Other Specialties", p. 26

grosso(a) big; thick

gruppo m group

guanti mpl gloves

guardare to watch; to look (at)

guardaroba f closet; cloakroom

guarnizione f garnishing

guasto(a) failure (mechanical); out of order

gubana: see section on "Regional Dishes", p. 53

guida f directory; guide; guidebook

guscio m shell

gustare to taste; to enjoy

gusto m taste; flavor

I.V.A. f V.A.T.

ieri yesterday

imbottigliato(a) bottled

imburrato(a) buttered

impanato(a) coated with breadcrumbs

impepata di cozze: see section on "Regional Dishes", p. 60

impermeabile m waterproof; raincoat

importante important

impossibile impossible

incinta pregnant

incluso(a) included; enclosed; inclusive

incontrare to meet

indicazioni fpl directions

indietro m backwards; back; behind

indirizzo m address

indivia f endive

informare to inform

informazioni fpl information

Inghilterra England

inglese English

ingresso m entry; entrance

inizio m start

innocuo(a) harmless

insaccati mpl sausages

insalata f salad

insalata di mare f seafood salad; see section on "National Dishes", p. 41

insalata di riso f rice salad; see section on "National Dishes", p. 41

insaporire to flavor; to season

insetto m insect

insieme together; outfit

integrale total; complete; wholemeal

interiora fpl entrails; offal

interno m inside; telephone extension; flat number

intero(a) whole

interurbana f long-distance call; toll-call

intingolo m sauce; tasty dish

intorno round

intossicazione alimentare f food poisoning

invece instead; but; instead of

inverno m winter

invitare to invite

involtini mpl stuffed meat rolls; see section on "National Dishes", p. 41 and section on "Basics", p. 27 and "Recipes", p. 65

involtini di pesce spada mpl

stuffed swordfish; see section on "Regional Dishes", p. 62
Irlanda Ireland
Italia Italy
italiano(a) Italian

lagane: see section on "Pasta", p. 14
lago m lake
Lambrusco: see section on "Wines", p. 18
lampascioni al forno: see section on "Regional Dishes", p. 61
lamponi mpl raspberries
lardo m lard; bacon fat
lasagne: see section on "Pasta", p. 14 and "National Dishes", p. 41
lasciare to leave; to let go of; to let
latte m milk
lattuga f lettuce
lavare to wash
lavoro m work
leggere to read
leggero(a) light
legumi mpl legumes
lente: lente a contatto f contact lens
lenticchie fpl lentils
lenticchie, zuppa di fpl lentil soup; see section on "National Dishes", p. 41
lepre f hare
lessato(a) boiled; stewed **lesso** m boiled meat
libero(a) free; clear; vacant
libro m book
lievito m yeast
limonata f lemonade
Limoncino: see section on

"Liqueurs", p. 21
limone m lemon
linea f line
lingua f tongue
liquore m liqueur
liscio(a) smooth; straight
lista f list
litro m liter
locale m room; place
Locorotondo: see "Wines", p. 19
lombata f loin
lontano far
luccio m pike
luce f light
luglio m July
lumache fpl snails
lunedì m Monday
lungo(a) long
luogo m place

maccarones con bottarga: see section on "Regional Dishes", p. 64
maccaruni di casa: see section on "Regional Dishes", p. 63
maccheroncini: see section on "Pasta", p. 14
maccheroni: see section on "Pasta", p. 14
maccheroni/pasta ai 4 formaggi: see section on "National Dishes", p. 41
maccheroni (or spaghetti) alla chitarra: see section on "Pasta", p. 14; see section on "Regional Dishes", p. 59
maccheroni al ferro: see section on "Pasta", p. 14
maccheroni alla norcina: see

section on "Regional Dishes", p. 58

macco di fave: see section on "Regional Dishes", p. 62

macedonia f fruit salad; see section on "National Dishes", p. 41

macelleria f butcher's shop

macinapepe m pepper-mill

macrobiotico macrobiotic

madre f mother

maggio m May

maggiorana f sweet marjoram

magro(a) thin; lean

mai never; ever

maiale m pig; pork

maiale alla brace m pork grilled on a spit; see section on "Regional Dishes", p. 64

maionese f mayonnaise

mais m maize; corn

malato(a) sick; ill

male m pain/ache **mal di stomaco/ mal di testa** stomachache/ headache

malinteso m misunderstanding

malloreddus: see section on "Regional Dishes", p. 64

Malvasia: see section on "Wines", p. 19

mancia f tip

mandarino m mandarin

mandorle fpl almonds

mangiare to eat

mano f hand

manzo m beef

mare m sea; seaside

mare-monti: see section on "Gastronomic Terms", p. 31

marinara: alla marinara: see section on "Gastronomic

Terms", p. 31

marinata f marinade

Marino: see section on "Wines", p. 19

marito m husband

marmellata f jam; marmalade

marroni mpl chestnuts

Marsala: see section on "Wines", p. 19

martedì m Tuesday

Martina Franca: see section on "Wines", p. 19

marzo m March

mascarpone: see section on "Cheeses", p. 9

masticare to chew

matita f pencil

mattina f morning

maturo(a) mature; ripe; age

medicina f medicine

medico m doctor

meglio m best; better

mela f apple

melanzana f eggplant

melanzane al funghetto: see section on "National Dishes", p. 42

melanzane alla campagnola: see section on "Regional Dishes", p. 61

melanzane alla parmigiana fpl eggplant in Parmesan cheese; see section on "National Dishes", p. 42

melanzane grigliate fpl grilled eggplant; see section on "National Dishes", p. 42

melanzane ripiene fpl stuffed eggplant ; see section on "National Dishes", p. 42 and "Regional Dishes", p. 60

melone m melon

melone al porto m melon with port; see section on "National Dishes", p. 42

meno less; minus

menta f mint

mentre while; whereas

menu m menu

mercato m market

mercoledì m Wednesday

merenda f snack

Meridione South of Italy

meringa f meringue

Merlot: see section on "Wines", p. 19

merluzzo m cod

mese m month

metà f half

metropolitana f underground train

mettere to put

mezzo m means; means of transport; middle

miele m honey

migliore better; best

Milano Milan

mille m thousand

millefoglie: see section on "National Dishes", p. 42

minestra f soup

minestra di fave m broadbean soup; see section on "Regional Dishes", p. 61

minestrone m vegetable soup; see section on "National Dishes", p. 42

Minestrone con il riso: see section on "Recipes", p. 65

minuto m minute

mirtilli mpl cranberries

Mirto: see section on "Liqueurs", p. 22

miscela f blend

misto(a) mix; mixed

modo m way; manner

moglie f wife

molluschi mpl molluscs

molto a lot; much; very

moneta f coin

monumenti mpl monuments

mortadella: see section on "Cold Cut Meats", p. 12

mosca f fly

Moscato: see section on "Wines", p. 19

mostarda: see section on "Other Specialties", p. 26

mostrare to show

mozzarella di bufala: see section on "Cheeses", p. 9

mozzarella fritta f fried mozzarella; see section on "National Dishes", p. 43

mozzarella in carrozza: see section on "National Dishes", p. 42 and "Recipes", p. 66

mugnaia: alla mugnaia: see section on "Gastronomic Terms", p. 31

muro m wall

museo m museum

musetto e brovade: see section on "Regional Dishes", p. 53

musica f music

Napoli Naples

nasello m hake

Natale m Christmas

Nebbiolo: see section on "Wines", p. 19

negozio m shop

nero(a) black

nessuno(a) no; nobody; none

niente nothing; anything

nocciole fpl hazlenuts

noce di cocco f coconut
noce moscata nutmeg
noci fpl walnuts; nuts
Nocino: see section on
 "Liqueurs", p. 22
noleggio m hire
nome m name
non-fumatore m non-smoker
nord m north
novembre m November
numero m number
nuotare to swim
Nuragus: see section on
 "Wines", p. 19

obbligatorio m compulsory;
 obligatory
oca f goose
occhiali mpl glasses
occhio m eye
occupato(a) busy; engaged
odore m smell; odor
oggi today
ogni every; each
Olanda Holland
olandese Dutch
oliera f cruet-stand
olio m oil
oliva f olive **olive nere / olive verdi**
 black olives/ green olives
olive all'ascolana: see section on
 "Regional Dishes", p. 56
Oltrepò Pavese: see section on
 "Wines", p. 19
ombrello m umbrella
omogeneizzato m baby food
ora f hour; now
orario m timetable; schedule
orata f sea-bream
orata alla barese: see section on
 "Regional Dishes", p. 61
ordinare to order

ordinazione f order
orecchiette: see section on
 "Pasta", p. 14
orecchiette alle cime di rapa:
 see section on "Regional
 Dishes", p. 61
orecchino m earring
origano m oregano; marjoram
oro m gold
orologio m watch; clock
ortaggi mpl vegetables
orto: dell'orto: see section on
 "Gastronomic Terms", p. 31
Orvieto: see section on
 "Wines", p. 19
orzetto: see section on
 "Regional Dishes", p. 52
orzo m barley
ospedale m hospital
ossibuchi: see section on
 "National Dishes", p. 43
ossibuchi in gremolada: see
 section on "Regional Dishes",
 p. 50
osso m bone
osteria f inn
ostriche fpl oysters
ottenere to get; to obtain
ottobre m October
ovoli mpl royal agaric

padella f frying pan
paesana: alla paesana: see
 section on "Gastronomic
 Terms", p. 31
paese m country; land
pagamento m payment
pagare to pay
pagello m sea-bream
paio m pair
pancarré m sandwich bread
pancetta/pancetta affumicata f

bacon; smoked bacon

pandispagna *m* sponge cake

pane *m* bread

pane frattau: see section on "Regional Dishes", p. 64

panforte: see section on "Sweets and Pastries", p. 24

pangrattato *m* breadcrumbs

panino *m* roll

paniscia/panissa: see section on "Regional Dishes", p. 48

panna *f* cream **panna liquida / panna montata** liquid cream/ whipped cream

panna cotta *f* cooked cream; see section on "National Dishes", p. 43

pannocchia *f* corn-on-the-cob

pansotti: see section on "Pasta", p. 14

pansotti al pesto di noci: see section on "Regional Dishes", p. 49

Panzanella: see section on "Regional Dishes", p. 55

panzerotti: see section on "National Dishes", p. 43

pappa al pomodoro *f* bread soup with tomatoes; see section on "Regional Dishes", p. 55

pappardelle: see section on "Pasta", p. 14

pappardelle alla lepre: see section on "Regional Dishes", p. 56

parcheggio *m* car park; parking lot (USA)

parco *m* park

pardulas: see section on "Regional Dishes", p. 64

parmigiana: alla parmigiana: see section on "Gastronomic

Terms", p. 32

parmigiana di melanzane: see section on "National Dishes", p. 43 and "Recipes", p. 67

parmigiano *m* Parmesan; hard tangy cheese often used in cooking

parmigiano reggiano: see section on "Cheeses", p. 9

parola *f* word

parrozzo: see section on "Regional Dishes", p. 59

parte *f* part; share; side

partire to go; to leave

Pasqua *f* Easter

passaporto *m* passport

passatelli: see section on "Regional Dishes", p. 54

passato/passato di verdura *m* cream of vegetable soup

pasta *f* pastry; pasta; dough

pasta al forno: see section on "National Dishes", p. 43

pasta al pomodoro: see section on "Recipes", p. 68

pasta alla Norma: see section on "Regional Dishes", p. 63

pasta allo scoglio: see section on "National Dishes", p. 43

pasta con le sarde *f* pasta with sardines; see section on "Regional Dishes", p. 63

pasta frolla *f* short crust pastry

pasta 'ncasciata: see section on "Regional Dishes", p. 63

pasta sfoglia *f* puff pastry

pastasciutta *f* pasta served in a sauce, not in a soup

paste: see section on "Sweets and Pastries", p. 24

pasticceria *f* cake shop

pasticcino *m* petit four

pasticcio: see section on

"Gastronomic Terms", p. 32
pasticcio di maccheroni: see section on "National Dishes", p. 43
pastiera: see section on "Regional Dishes", p. 60
pastiglia *f* tablet; lozenge
pastina *f* noodles
pasto *m* meal
patate potatoes **patate fritte/patate lesse/patate arrosto** *fpl* chips/ boiled/ roast
patatine *fpl* crisps
pecorino: see section on "Cheeses", p. 10
pelare to remove the hair from; to pluck
penna *f* pen; quill-shaped tube of pasta
penne: see section on "Pasta", p. 14
pennette: see section on "Pasta", p. 14
pentola *f* pot
pepe *m* pepper
peperonata: see section on "National Dishes", p. 44 and "Recipes", p. 68
peperoncino *m* chili pepper
peperone *m* pepper (vegetable)
peperoni arrostiti *mpl* roast peppers; see section on "National Dishes", p. 44
per for; per; in order to
pera *f* pear
perché why; because; in order that
perdere to lose
permesso *m* permission; permit
pesante heavy
pesca *f* peach; angling; fishing
pescatora: alla pescatora: see

section on "Gastronomic Terms", p. 32
pesce *m* fish
pesce al cartoccio: see section on "National Dishes", p. 44
pesce al salmoriglio: see section on "Regional Dishes", p. 63
pesce persico *m* perch
pesce spada *m* swordfish
pesce spada alla ghiotta: see section on "Regional Dishes", p. 63
pesto alla genovese: see section on "Basics", p. 27
petto *m* breast; chest
pezzo *m* piece; cut (of meat)
piacere *m* enjoyment; pleasure; to please
piadina: see section on "Other Specialties", p. 26
piano *m* slowly; quietly; floor; plan
pianta *f* map
piatto *m* dish; course; plate
piazza *f* square
piccante spicy; hot
piccata/scaloppina al Marsala: see section on "National Dishes", p. 44
piccione *m* pigeon
piccolo(a) small; little
pici: see section on "Pasta", p. 14 and "Regional Dishes", p. 56
piedi /a piedi *mpl* feet/ on foot
pieno(a) full
pietanza *f* dish; main course
pillola *f* pill
pinoli *mpl* pine kernels
Pinot: see section on "Wines", p. 19
pinza: see section on "Regional

Dishes", p. 52
piscina *f* swimming pool
piselli *mpl* peas
pistacchi *mpl* pistachio nuts
più more; most; plus
pizza: see section on "National Dishes", p. 44
pizza al formaggio: see section on "Regional Dishes", p. 57
pizza capricciosa: see section on "National Dishes", p. 44
pizza Margherita: see section on "National Dishes", p. 44 and "Recipes", p. 69
pizza napoletana: see section on "National Dishes", p. 44
pizza 4 stagioni: see section on "National Dishes", p. 44
pizzaiola: alla pizzaiola: see section on "Gastronomic Terms", p. 32
pizzoccheri alla valtellinese: see section on "Regional Dishes", p. 50
poco(a) little; not much
poi then
polenta: see section on "Basics", p. 27
polenta concia: see section on "Regional Dishes", p. 49
polenta e osei: see section on "Regional Dishes", p. 50
polipi/polipetti affogati: see section on "National Dishes", p. 45
polipo *m* polyp; octopus
pollo *m* chicken
pollo alla cacciatora *m* chicken cacciatore; see section on "National Dishes", p. 44 and "Recipes", p. 70
pollo alla diavola: see section on

"National Dishes", p. 45
pollo alla marengo: see section on "National Dishes", p. 45
pollo alla romana: see section on "Regional Dishes", p. 58
polpa *f* pulp; flesh
polpette *fpl* meatballs; see section on "Basics", p. 27
pomodori al riso *mpl* tomatoes with rice; see section on "Regional Dishes", p. 58
pomodoro *m* tomato
pompelmo *m* grapefruit
porchetta: see section on "Other Specialties", p. 26
porchetta alla perugina: see section on "Regional Dishes", p. 57
porcini *mpl* mushrooms
porri *mpl* leeks
porta *f* door
portacenere *m* ashtray
portafoglio *m* wallet
portare to bring; to carry; to wear
porzione *f* portion; helping
posate *fpl* cutlery
possibile possible
posto *m* place; position; job; seat
potere can; to be able; to be allowed; power
pranzo *m* lunch
preferire to prefer
prego don't mention it! it's a pleasure! you're welcome
prendere to take
prenotare to book; to reserve
prenotazione *f* reservation
preparare to prepare
presnitz: see section on "Regional Dishes", p. 53

prezzemolo *m* parsley
prezzo *m* price
prima first
primizie *fpl* first fruits or vegetables
profiteroles: see section on "National Dishes", p. 45
pronto(a) ready; hello
proprio just; really; own
prosciutto *m* ham: see section on "Cold Cut Meats", p. 12
prosciutto e melone *m* ham and melon; see section on "National Dishes", p. 45
Prosecco di Valdobbiadene: see section on "Wines", p. 20
provare to try
provolone: see section on "Cheeses", p. 10
prugne *fpl* plums
pulito(a) clean
puntarelle all'acciuga: see section on "Regional Dishes", p. 58
purè *m* purée

quaglia *f* quail
qualche some
qualcosa something; anything
qualcuno somebody; anybody
quale what; which; which one
qualsiasi any
quando when
quanto(a) how much; how many
quarto(a) quarter; fourth
quasi nearly; almost
quello(a) that
questo(a) this
qui here

radicchio *m* chicory
radicchio di Treviso alla griglia: see section on "National Dishes", p. 45
radio *f* radio
raffreddare to cool; to make cool
ragazza/ragazzo *m/f* girl/ boy
ragù (or **Bolognese sauce**) *m* meat sauce; see section "Basics", p. 27
rape *fpl* turnips
ravanelli *mpl* radishes
ravioli: see section on "Pasta", p. 14 and "National Dishes", p. 45
ravioli all'anconetana: see section on "Regional Dishes", p. 56
reclamo *m* complaint
regione *f* region
restare to stay; to remain; to be left
resto *m* remainder; change
ribes *m* blackcurrant
ribollita: see section on "Regional Dishes", p. 56
ricetta *f* prescription; recipe
ricevuta *f* receipt
ricotta: see section on "Cheeses", p. 10
rigatoni: see section on "Pasta", p. 14
rigatoni con la pajata: see section on "Regional Dishes", p. 58
rimanere to stay; to remain; to be left
rimborso *m* refund
ringraziare to thank
ripieno [as a noun or adj.] *m* stuffing; stuffed; filled
riscaldamento *m* heating
riscaldare to heat

riservare to reserve
riservato(a) reserved
risi e bisi: see section on "Regional Dishes", p. 52
riso *m* laugh; rice
riso alla pilota: see section on "Regional Dishes", p. 50
risotto: see section on "Basics", p. 27
risotto agli scampi: see section on "National Dishes", p. 45
risotto ai funghi: see section on "National Dishes", p. 45
risotto al nero di seppia: see section on "National Dishes", p. 46
risotto alla certosina: see section on "Regional Dishes", p. 51
risotto alla milanese: see section on "National Dishes", p. 46 and "Recipes", p. 70
risotto alla pescatora: see section on "National Dishes", p. 46
rispondere to answer; to reply; to respond
ristorante *m* restaurant
ritardo *m* delay
ritorno *m* return
robiola: see section on "Cheeses", p. 10
rognone *m* kidney
Roma Rome
rombo *m* turbot
rompere to break
rosmarino *m* rosemary
rosso(a) red
rosticceria *f* shop selling roast meat and other prepared food
rostone: see section on "Regional Dishes", p. 49

rotto(a) broken
rucola *f* type of Roman lettuce with a strong flavor
rumore *m* noise
rumoroso(a) noisy
rustico(a) rural; country

sabato *m* Saturday
sala *f* hall; auditorium
salame: see section on "Cold Cut Meats", p. 12
salatini *mpl* cocktail snacks
salato(a) salted; salty; savory
sale *m* salt
saliera *f* salt shaker
salire to rise; to go up
salmone *m* salmon **salmone affumicato** smoked salmon
salsa *f* sauce; gravy
salsicce con patate *fpl* sausages with potatoes; see section on "National Dishes", p. 46
salsiccia *f* sausage
saltimbocca alla romana: see section on "Regional Dishes", p. 58 and "Recipes", p. 71
salumi *mpl* cured pork meats
salvia *f* sage
Sambuca: see section on "Liqueurs", p. 22
Sangiovese: see section on "Wines", p. 20
sangue: al sangue: see section on "Gastronomic Terms", p. 32
sapere to know
sapone *m* soap
sapore *m* flavor; taste
saporito(a) flavorful
sarago *m* bream
sarde a beccafico: see section on "Regional Dishes", p. 63
sarde a scapece: see section on

"Regional Dishes", p. 62
Sardegna Sardinia
sardine *fpl* sardines
sartù di riso: see section on "Regional Dishes", p. 60
Sassolino: see section on "Liqueurs", p. 22
sbaglio *m* mistake
sbucciare to peel
scaldare to warm
scale *fpl* stairs
scaloppa or **scaloppe:** see section on "Basics", p. 28 and "National Dishes", p. 46
scaloppine alla bolognese: see section on "Regional Dishes", p. 54
scamorza ai ferri: see section on "Regional Dishes", p. 59
scampi *mpl* scampi
scatola *f* box
schiaccianoci *m* (pair of) nutcrackers
sciroppato(a) in syrup
sciroppo *m* syrup
scomodo(a) uncomfortable; awkward
scrippelle: see section on "Regional Dishes", p. 59
scrivere to write
scuro(a) dark
secco(a) dry; dried
secondo(a) second; according to
sedano *m* celery
sedia *f* chair
seggiolone *m* high chair
selvaggina *f* game (hunting)
semifreddo *m* chilled dessert made with ice-cream; see section on "National Dishes", p. 46
semolino *m* semolina

semplice simple
sempre always; ever
senape *f* mustard
sentire to feel; to hear
senza without
seppie *fpl* cuttlefish
sera *f* evening
servizio *m* service; service charge
sete *f* thirst
settembre *m* September
settimana *f* week
sfogliatelle ricce: see section on "Sweets and Pastries", p. 24
sformato timbale; pudding; shapeless; disfigured
sgombro *m* mackerel
sgrassare to remove grease from; to scour
sgusciare to slip; to shell (peas)
Sicilia Sicily
sigaretta *f* cigarette
sigaro *m* cigar
significare to mean **cosa significa?** what does it mean?
signora *f* lady; madam, Mrs.
signore *m* gentleman; sir; Mr.
signorina *f* young woman; Miss
smacafam: see section on "Regional Dishes", p. 52
Soave: see section on "Wines", p. 20
sodo hard; hard-boiled
soffritto *m* slightly fried or browned onions
sogliola *f* sole
soia *f* soya
solamente only
solo only
soppressa: see section on "Cold Cut Meats", p. 13
soppressata: see section on

"Cold Cut Meats", p. 13

sopra on; above; over; on top

sorbetto *m* sorbet; sherbet; see section "National Dishes", p. 46

sott'olio in oil

sottaceti *mpl* pickles

sottile thin; fine; subtle

sotto underneath; under; below

spaghetti: see section on "Pasta", p. 14

spaghetti aglio, olio e peperoncino: see section on "National Dishes", p. 46 and "Recipes", p. 72

spaghetti alla carbonara: see section on "Recipes", p. 72

spaghetti alla checca: see section on "Regional Dishes", p. 58 and "Recipes", p. 72

spaghetti alla gricia: see section on "Regional Dishes", p. 59

spaghetti alla puttanesca: see section on "Regional Dishes", p. 60

spaghetti alle vongole *mpl* see section on "National Dishes", p. 46

spaghetti cacio e pepe: see section on "Regional Dishes", p. 59

spaghetti/fettuccine al tartufo spaghetti with truffles: see section on "Regional Dishes", p. 57

spalla *f* shoulder

spazzola *f* brush

speck: see section on "Cold Cut Meats", p. 13

spegnere to turn off; to put out

spesa *f* expense

spesso often

spettacolo *m* show; performance

spezie *fpl* spices

spezzatino *m* stew; see section on "Basics", p. 28

spiccioli *mpl* (small) change

spiedini *mpl* skewers

spiedo *m* spit

spigola *f* bass

spilla di sicurezza *f* safety pin

spinaci *mpl* spinach

spongata: see section on "Sweets and Pastries", p. 24

sporco(a) dirty

spremuta *f* freshly squeezed juice

Spumante: see section on "Wines", p. 20

spuntino *m* snack

stagionato(a) ripe; mature

stagione *f* season

stanza *f* room

stappare to uncork; to uncap

stasera tonight

Stati Uniti (d'America) *mpl* United States (of America)

stazione *f* station; resort

stecchino *m* toothpick; wooden skewer

stesso(a) same

stinco di maiale *m* pork shin bone; see section on "National Dishes", p. 52

stoccafisso in potacchio: see section on "Regional Dishes", p. 56

stracchino: see section on "Cheeses", p. 10

stracciatella: see section on "Regional Dishes", p. 59

strada *f* road; street

strangolapreti: see section on "Regional Dishes", p. 52

straniero(a) foreign; foreigner; overseas

Strega: see section on

"Liqueurs", p. 22
stretto(a) narrow; tight; strait (sea)
strudel di mele m apple strudel; see section on "National Dishes", p. 53
strutto m lard
stufato m stew; see section on "National Dishes", p. 51
stuzzicadenti mpl toothpicks
stuzzichini mpl appetizers
subito at once
succedere to happen; **cosa è successo?** what happened?
succo m juice
sud m south
sugo m sauce; gravy; juice
suino m pork meats
superalcolici mpl high-proof spirits
supplì: see section on "National Dishes", p. 47
surgelato(a) frozen
svenuto(a) fainted
Svizzera Switzerland

tabaccheria f tobacconist's shop
tacchino m turkey
tacchino alla melagrana: see section on "Regional Dishes", p. 52
tagliare to cut
tagliatelle: see section on "Pasta", p. 14
tagliatelle al ragù: see section on "Recipes", p. 73
tagliolini: see section on "Pasta", p. 14
tajarin: see section on "Regional Dishes", p. 49
taleggio: see section on "Cheeses", p. 10
tappo m stopper

tartine fpl canapé
tartufo m truffle; chocolate truffle; see section on "Other Specialties", p. 26
tavola or **tavolo** f/m table **tavola calda** f snack bar
tazza / tazzina f cup/ coffee cup
tè m tea
tedesco(a) German
tegame m frying pan
telefonata f phone call
telefono m telephone
telline fpl clams
temperatura f temperature **temperatura ambiente** room temperature
tempo m time
tenere to hold; to keep
tenero(a) tender
Teroldego: see section on "Wines", p. 20
terrazza f terrace
terrina f tureen
tiella di riso: see section on "Regional Dishes", p. 61
timballo: see section on "Basics", p. 28
timo m thyme
tiramisù: see section on "National Dishes", p. 47 and "Recipes", p. 74
tisana f infusion
togliere to remove; to take away
tonnarelli: see section on "Pasta", p. 14
tonno m tuna fish
Torino Turin
tornare to come/go back; to return
torrone: see section on "Sweets and Pastries", p. 24
torta di riso/degli addobbi: see

section on "National Dishes",
p. 54

torta f cake; tart; pie

torta gianduia: see section on
"Regional Dishes", p. 49

torta pasqualina: see section on
"Regional Dishes", p. 49

torta salata/rustica: see section
on "National Dishes", p. 47

torta sbrisolona: see section on
"Regional Dishes", p. 51

tortelli: see section on "Pasta",
p. 14

tortelli di zucca: see section on
"Regional Dishes", p. 51

tortelli verdi: see section on
"Regional Dishes", p. 54

tortellini: see section on "Pasta",
p. 14

tortiera di alici: see section on
"Regional Dishes", p. 61

tortiglioni: see section on
"Pasta", p. 14

tortino m pie

tostato(a) toasted

tovaglia f table-cloth

tovagliolo m napkin; serviette

tramezzino m sandwich

tranne except for

trasporto m transport **mezzi di
trasporto** means of transport

trattaliu: see section on
"Regional Dishes", p. 64

trattoria f inn; restaurant

Trebbiano: see section on
"Wines", p. 20

trenette al pesto: see section on
"Regional Dishes", p. 50

treno m train

trifolati: see section on
"Gastronomic Terms", p. 32

triglie fpl mullet

triglie alla livornese: see section
on "Regional Dishes", p. 56

trippa f tripe; see section on
"National Dishes", p. 47

tritato(a) minced; chopped

troppo too much; too

trota f trout

trota salmonata f sea trout; see
section on "National Dishes",
p. 53

trovare to find

tuorlo m yolk

tutto(a) everything; all

uguale equal; same

ultimo(a) last

umido: in umido: see section on
"Gastronomic Terms", p. 32

unto(a) greasy; oily

uovo m egg **uova sode / uova
strapazzate / uova al burro** boiled
egg/ scrambled egg/ egg fried
in butter

usare to use

uscire to go out; to come out

uscita f exit

uva f grapes

uvetta f raisins

vacanza f holiday(s)

valdostana: alla valdostana: see
section on "Gastronomic
Terms", p. 32

valigia f suitcase

Valpolicella: see section on
"Wines", p. 20

valuta f currency

vaniglia f vanilla

vapore: al vapore m steam;
steamed

vassoio m tray

vecchio(a) old

vedere to see
veduta f view; sight
vegetariano(a) vegetarian; see section on "Gastronomic Terms", p. 32
veloce fast; quick
velocemente quickly
vendere to sell
venerdì f Friday
Venezia Venice
venire to come
verde green
Verdicchio di Jesi: see section on "Wines", p. 20
verdura f vegetables
Vermentino di Gallura: see section on "Wines", p. 20
vermicelli: see section on "Pasta", p. 14
vermicelli alla siracusana: see section on "Regional Dishes", p. 63
Vermouth: see section on "Liqueurs", p. 22
Vernaccia: see section on "Wines", p. 20
verso toward(s)
verza f savoy cabbage
vespa f wasp
vetro m glass
via f street; by way of
Vin santo: see section on "Wines", p. 20
vincisgrassi: see section on "Regional Dishes", p. 56
vino m wine **bianco / rosato / rosso / leggero / robusto** white/ rosé/ red/ light/ full-bodied
Vino nobile di Montepulciano: see section on "Wines", p. 20
vitamine fpl vitamins
vitello m veal; calf

vitello tonnato m veal with tuna; see section on "National Dishes", p. 47 and "Recipes", p. 75
volere to want
volo m flight
vongole fpl clams
vuoto(a) empty

würstel m frankfurter; Vienna sausage

zabaione: see section on "Basics", p. 28 and "Recipes", p. 75
zafferano m saffron
zampone: see section on "Cold Cut Meats", p. 13
zanzare fpl mosquitoes
zelten: see section on "Regional Dishes", p. 53
zenzero m ginger
zite: see section on "Pasta", p. 14
zucca f pumpkin; marrow
zuccheriera f sugar-bowl
zucchero m sugar
zucchine fpl zucchini
zuccotto: see section on "National Dishes", p. 47
zuppa f soup
zuppa di farro: see section on "Regional Dishes", p. 56
zuppa di pesce f fish soup; see section on "National Dishes", p. 47
zuppa di pesce di Maratea: see section on "Regional Dishes", p. 62
zuppa inglese: see section on "National Dishes", p. 47 and "Recipes", p. 75

GASTRONOMIC DICTIONARY

ENGLISH-ITALIAN

able, to be potere po-_tayray_
above sopra _sohpra_
according to secondo
  say-_kohndo_
account conto _kohntoh_
ache male _mahlay_
acid acido _a_-chee-do
additive additivo ad-dee-_tee_-vo
address indirizzo eendee-_reets_-so
adult adulto a-_doolto_
aeroplane aereo a-e-_ray_-o
after dopo _dohpoh_
afterward(s) dopo _dohpoh_
against contro _kohn_-troh
age età ay-_tah_
ahead avanti _avan_-tee
air aria _ahree_-a
air conditioning aria condizionata _ahree_-a kohndeets-yoh-
  nahta
airport aeroporto a-ay-ropor-to
à la carte alla carta _al_-la _karta_
a lot molto _mohlto_
alcoholic alcolico _alko_-leeko
alcoholic drinks alcolici a_lko_-lee-
  chee
alert attento at-_ten_-to
all tutto(a) _toot_-to/a
allergy allergia al-layr-_jee_-ah
allowed permesso payr-_mays_-so
almonds mandorle _mandor_-lay
almost quasi _kwahzee_
also anche _ankay_
always sempre _saympray_
American coffee caffè lungo
  kaf-_fe_ _loon_-go;
among(st) fra _fra_
anchovy acciuga at-_choo_-ga
angle angolo _an_-golo
angling pesca _payska_
anise anice _a_-nee-chay
announcement comunicazione

kohmoon-ee-kats-_yoh_-nay
answer, to rispondere ree-_spon_-
  dayray
antibiotic antibiotico _antee_-bee-
  oteeko
any qualsiasi kwal-_see_-a-see
anybody qualcuno kwal-_koono_
anything qualcosa kwal-_koza_
aperitif aperitivo a-payree-_teevo_
appetite/enjoy your meal appetito ap-pay-_teeto_/buon appetito
  bwon a-pay-_teeto_
appetizer antipasto an-tee-_pasto_
appetizers stuzzichini stoots-see-
  keenee
apple mela _mayla_
application (job) domanda do-
  manda
appointment appuntamento ap-
  poonta-_maynto_
apricot albicocca albee-_kok_-ka
April aprile _apree_-lay
aroma/fragrances aroma/aromi
  a-_roma_/a-_ro_-mee
aromatic aromatico a-ro-_mattee_-
  ko
arrive, to arrivare ar-ree-_vahray_
artichoke carciofo kar-_chohfo_
as come _kohmay_
as far as fino a _feeno_ a
as well anche _ankay_
ash(es) cenere _chay_-nayray
ashtray portacenere _porta_-_chay_-
  nayray
ask, to chiedere kee_ay_-dayray
asparagus asparagi _aspa_-rajee
aspirin aspirina aspee-_reena_
at least almeno al-_may_-no
attentive attento at-_ten_-to
aubergine melanzana
  mayland-_zahna_
August agosto a_gos_-to

Austria Austria _owstree-a_
Austrian austriaco _owstree-ako_
authentic autentico _owten-teeko_
avocado avocado _avo-kahdo_
avoid, to evitare _ay-vee-tahray_
awkward scomodo(a) _sko-modo_

back indietro _een-dee-etro_
backwards indietro _een-dee-etro_
bacon pancetta _panchayt-ta_
bad brutto(a) _broot-to/a;_ cattivo(a) _ka-teevo/a_
bag borsa _borsa_
baking cottura _koht-toora_
banana banana _ba-nana_
bank banca _banka_
bar bar _bar_
barley orzo _or-dzo_
barman barista _bar-eesta_
basil basilico _ba-zeel-eeko_
bass branzino _bran-tsee-no;_ spigola _spee-gola_
bath bagno _ban-yo_
bay leaf alloro
Bavarian bavarese _ba-va-rayzay_
be careful attento _at-ten-to_
be enough, to bastare _ba-staray_
be left, to restare _ray-stahray_
be sufficient, to bastare _ba-staray_
beans fagioli _fa-jolee_
beat frullare _frool-lahray_
beautiful bello(a) _bel-lo_
because perché _payrkay_
beef manzo _man-zo_
beer birra _beer-ra_
beet bietole _bee-ay-to-lay_
beetroot barbabietola _bahr-bab-yetola_
behind dietro _dee-etro;_ indietro _een-dee-etro_
below sotto _soht-to_
berry bacca _bak-ka_

beside accanto a _ak-kanto a_
best migliore _meel-yohray_
better meglio _mel-yo_
between fra _fra_
big grande _granday;_ grosso/a _gros-so/a_
bill conto _kohntoh_
biscuits biscotti _bee-skot-tee_
bitter acerbo _a-chayr-bo;_ agro _agro;_ amaro _a-mahro_
bitter liqueur amaretto _a-mah-rayt-to_
bittersweet agrodolce _agro-dol-chay_
black nero(a) _nayro/a_
blackcurrant ribes _reebes_
blend miscela _mee-shay-la_
blouse camicetta _ka-meecheta_
boil, to bollire _bol-leeray_
boiled bollito _bol-leeto;_ lessato _lays-sah-to_
boiled eggs uova sode _wova soday_
boiling bollente _bol-lentay_
bone osso _os-so_
book libro _leebro_
bottle bottiglia _bot-teel-ya_
bottled imbottigliato(a) _eem-bot-teel-yato/a_
bottle-opener apribottiglie _apree-bot-teel-yay_
bouillon cube dado _da-do_
bovine bovino _bo-veeno_
box cassa _kas-sa;_ scatola _skah-tola_
boy ragazzo _ragats-so_
brain cervella/cervello _chayr-vel-la/o_
braised brasato _bra-za-to_
brandy acquavite _akwa-vee-tay_
bread pane _pahnay_
breadcrumbs pangrattato _pan-grat-tah-to_

break, to rompere *rom-payray*
breakfast colazione *kola-tsyohnay*
bream sarago *sa-rago*
breast petto *payt-to*
bring, to portare *por-tahray*
broad beans fave *fah-vay*
broccoli broccoli *brok-kolee*
broken rotto(a) *roht-to(a)*
browned dorato(a) *do-rato*
brush spazzola *spats-sola*
Brussels sprouts cavolini di Bruxelles *kahvo-leen-nee dee brooksel*
buds germogli *jayr-mol-yee*
burn, to bruciare *broo-cha-ray*
burnt bruciato(a) *broo-cha-to/a*
bus autobus *ow-toboos*
busy occupato(a) *ok-koo-pahto/a*
but ma *mah*
butcher's macelleria *mah-chayl-lay-ree-a*
butter burro *boor-ro*
buttered imburrato(a) *eem-boor-rato/a*
button bottone *bot-tohnay*
buy, to comprare *kom-prahray*
by way of via *vee-a*

cabbage cavolo *kah-volo*
cake torta *tor-ta*
cake shop pasticceria *pas-tee-chay-ree-a*
calf vitello *veetayl-lo*
call, to chiamare *keea-mahray*
calm calmo(a) *kalmo/a*
calming calmante *kal-mantay*
calories calorie *kal-lo-reeay*
camomile camomilla *kamo-meel-la*
campaign campagna *kampan-ya*
can potere *po-tayray*
canapé tartine *tahr-teenay*
cancel, to cancellare *kanchayl-*

lahray; disdire *dees-deeray*
candied canditi *kan-dee-tee*
candle candela *kan-dayla*
candy caramella *kara-mella*
capers capperi *kapper-ee*
capon cappone *kappon-ay*
car automobile *owto-mo-bee-lay*
car park parcheggio *parkayd-jo*
carafe caraffa *karaf-fa*
caramel caramello *kara-mel-lo*
cardoons cardi *kar-dee*
care-taker custode *koo-stoday*
carrot carota *ka-rota*
carry, to portare *por-tahray*
cash contante *kon-tantee*;
cash desk cassa *kas-sa*
cashier cassiere *kas-see-ay-ray*
cauliflower cavolfiore *kahvol-fyohray*
caviar caviale *kav-ya-lay*
celery sedano *se-dano*
cellar cantina *kan-tee-na*
center centro *chentro*
central centrale *chayn-trahlay*
cereals cereali *chayray-ahlee*
chair sedia *sed-ya*
champagne champagne *sham-pan-ye*
change cambio *kambyo*; resto *ray-sto*
change, to cambiare *kamb-yahray*
chard biete *bee-aytay*
charge, to addebitare *ad-daybee-tahray*
cheap economico/a *ayko-no-meeko/a*
check, to controllare *kontrol-lahray*
check-out cassa *kas-sa*
cheese formaggio *formad-jo*
chemist shop farmacia *farma-chee-a*
check assegno *as-sayn-yo*

cherry ciliegia *chee-lee-ayja*
chest petto *payt-to*
chestnuts castagne *kastan-yay*;
marroni *mar-rohnnee*
chew, to masticare
ma-stee-kahray
chick-peas ceci *chay-chee*
chicken pollo *pohl-lo*
chicken leg coscia di pollo
kosh-a dee pohl- lo
chicory cicoria *cheek-oree-a*;
radicchio *ra-deek-kyo*
child bambino(a) *bam-beeno/a*
chili pepper peperoncino *pay-pay-ron-cheeno*
chocolate cioccolata *chok-ko-lahta*
chocolates cioccolatini *chok-kola-teenee*
chop (meat) braciola *bra-cho-la*
chop, to tritare *tree-tahray*
chopped tritato *tree-tahto*
Christmas Natale *na-tahlay*
cigar sigaro *see-garo*
cigarette sigaretta *seega-rayt-ta*
cinnamon cannella *kan-nel-la*
citron cedro *chedro*
citrus fruit agrume *a-groo-may*
city città *cheet-ta*
clams telline *tayl-leenay*; vongole
vong-golay
clean pulito(a) *poo-lee-to/a*
clear chiaro(a) *keea-ro*; libero(a)
lee-bay-ro/a
client cliente *klee-entay*
cloakroom guardaroba *gwarda-roba*
clock orologio *oro-lojo*
close, to chiudere *keeoo-dayray*;
fermare *fayr-mahray*
closed chiuso(a) *kee-oozo/a*
closure chiusura *keeoo-zoo-ra*

coat cappotto *kap-potto*
cockrel galletto *gal-letto*
cocoa cacao *kaka-o*
coconut cocco *kok-ko*
cod merluzzo *mayr-loo-tso*
coffee caffè *kaf-fe*; espresso
aysprays-so
coffee with a dash of milk caffè
macchiato *kaf-fe mak-ya-to*
coin moneta *mo-nayta*
cold freddo(a) *frayd-do/a*
color colore *ko-lohray*
coloring coloranti *ko-loh-rantee*
come, to venire *vay-neeray*
comfortable comodo *ko-modo*
communication comunicazione
kohmoon-ee-kats-yoh-nay
company comitiva *koh-meeteeva*
complaint reclamo *ray-klahmo*
complete integrale *een-tay-gralay*
compulsory obbligatorio *ob-bleega-tor-yo*
conclusion fine *feenay*
cone cono *kohno*
confirm, to confermare *konfayr-mahray*
contact lenses lenti a contatto
lentee a kontat-to
continue, to continuare *kon-tee-noo-ahray*
control, to controllare *kontrol-lahray*
convenient comodo *ko-modo*
cook cuoco(a) *kwoh-ko*
cook, to cucinare *koochee-nahray*
cooked cotto(a) *koht-to*
cooking cottura *koht-toora*
cool fresco(a) *fraysko/a*
cool, to raffreddare *raf-frayddah-ray*
Coquille St Jacques (scallop)
capesante *kap-pay-san-tay*

corn mais *ma-ees*
corner angolo *an-golo*
corn-on-the-cob pannocchia *pan-nok-kya*
cost costo *kosto*
cost, to costare *kos-tahray*
cotton cotone *ko-tohnay*
country paese *pah-ay-say*
countryside campagna *kampan-ya*
courgettes zucchine *dsook-keenay*
course piatto *pee-at-to*
cover, to coprire *ko-preeray*
crab granchio *grank-yo*
cranberries mirtilli *meer-teel-lee*
crayfish aragosta *ara-gosta*
cream crema *cray-ma*; panna *pan-na*
creampuff bignè *been-ye*
credit card carta di credito *karta dee kray-dee-to*
crisp croccante *krok-kant-tay*
crisps patatine *pata-teenay*
croissant cornetto *kohr-nayt-to*
croquettes crocchette *krok-kayt-tay*
crouton crostini *kros-tee-nee*
crowded affollato *af-fol-lahto*
cucumber cetriolo *chaytree-olo*
cummin cumino *koo-meeno*
cup tazza *tats-sa*
currency valuta *va-loota*
cushion cuscino *koo-sheeno*
customer cliente *klee-entay*
cut, to tagliare *tal-yahray*
cutlery posate *po-zahtay*
cutlet costoletta/cotoletta *kos-to-laytta/ko-to-layt-ta*
cuttlefish seppie *say-peeay*

dance, to ballare *bal-lahray*
dark scuro(a) *skooro/a*

date appuntamento *ap-poonta-maynto*
dates (fruit) datteri *dat-tay-ree*
daughter figlia *feel-ya*
day giorno/giornata *jorno/jor-nah-tah*
dear caro(a) *karo/a*
debit, to addebitare *ad-day-bee-tahray*
decaffeinated decaffeinato *day-kaf-fay-ee-nato*
decanter caraffa *karaf-fa*
December dicembre *deechem-bray*
decorated decorato(a) *day-koh-rah-to*
delay ritardo *ree-tahrdo*
dentures dentiera *dayn-tee-ay-ra*
deposit, to depositare *daypo-zee-tahray*
dessert dessert *day-sayrt;* dolce *dolchay*
diabetic diabetico(a) *deea-be-teeko*
diet dieta *dee-eta*
different diverso(a) *dee-vayrso*
difficult difficile *deef-fee-cheelay*
digestible digeribile *dee-je-ree-beelay*
digestive digestivo *dee-jes-tee-vo*
dinner cena *chayna*
direction direzione *deerayts-yonay*
directions indicazioni *een-dee-kats-yohnee*
director direttore *deerayttohr-ray*
directory guida *gweeda*
dirty sporco(a) *sporko/a*
disabled disabile *dees-abeel-lay*
discothèque discoteca *deesko-teka*
dish/tub coppa/coppetta *kop-pa/kop-payt-tah*
disinfect, to disinfettare *deezeen-*

fayt-_taray_
disinfectant disinfettante _dee-zeen-fayt-_tantay__
distance distanza _deestan-tsa_
distributor distributore _dees-tree-boo-toray_
disturb, to disturbare _dees-toor-baray_
do, to fare _fahray_
doctor medico _me-deeko_
documents documenti _dokoo-mayntee_
dollars dollari _dol-laree_
door porta _porta_
double doppio(a) _dop-yo_
dough pasta _pasta_
doughnut bombolone _bom-bo-lo-nay_
down/downstairs giù _joo_
draught beer birra alla spina _beer-ra al-la spee-na_
dressing condimento _kondee-maynto_
dried secco(a) _sayk-ko_
dried fruit frutta secca _froot-ta sayk-ka_
dried mushrooms funghi secchi _foongee sayk- kee_
drink bevanda _bayvan-da;_ bibita _bee-beeta_
drink, to bere _bayray_
dry secco(a) _sayk-ko/a_
duck anatra _a-natra_
Dutch olandese _o-lan-dayzay_

each ogni _on-yee_
earring orecchino _orayk-keeno_
Easter Pasqua _paskwa_
easy facile _fa-cheelay_
eat, to mangiare _man-jahray_
economical economico(a) _ayko-no-meeko/a_

E.E.C.(European Economic Community) CEE _chay_
eel anguilla _angweel-la_
egg uovo _wovo;_
eggwhite albume _al-boomay_
eggs fried in butter uova al burro _wova al boor-ro_
eggplant melanzana _mayland-zahna_
elevator ascensore _ashayn-sohray_
embassy ambasciata _amba-shahta_
empty vuoto(a) _vwoto/a_
enclosed incluso(a) _een-kloo-zo/a_
end fine _feenay_
endive indivia _een-dee-veea_
engaged occupato(a) _ok-koo-pahto/a_
England Inghilterra _eengeel-ter-ra_
English inglese _een-glayzay_
enjoyment piacere _pee-a-chayray_
enough abbastanza _ab-bas-tansa_
enter, to entrare _ayn-trahray_
entrance entrata _ayn-trahta;_ ingresso _eengres-so_
entry ingresso _eengres-so_
envelope busta _boo-sta_
equal uguale _oo-gwal-lay_
error errore _ayr-rohray_
etiquette etichetta _ay-tee-kaytta_
evening sera _sayra_
ever mai _ma-ee;_ sempre _saym-pray_
every ogni _on-yee_
everything tutto(a) _toot-to/a_
except for tranne _tran-nay_
exchange cambio _kambyo_
excursion escursione _ayskoors-yohnay;_ gita _jee-ta_
exit uscita _oo-sheeta_
expense spesa _spay-za_
expensive costoso(a) _kohs-tohzo_

experienced esperto(a) *ay-spayr-to/a*
expert esperto(a) *ay-spayrto/a*
express espresso *aysprays-so*
external esterno *ay-ster-no*
extract estratto *ay-strat-to*
eye occhio *ok-yo*

failure (mechanical) guasto(a) *gwasto*
fainted svenuto(a) *zvay-nooto*
fall, to cadere *ka-dayray*
familiar familiare *fameel-ya-ray*
family famiglia *fameel-ya*
famous famoso(a) *fa-mohzo*
far lontano *lon-tahno*
fast veloce *vay-lohchay*
fat grasso(a) *gras-so/a*
favor favore *fa-vohray*
February febbraio *feb-bra-yo*
feeding alimentazione *alee-mayn-tahts-yo-nay*
feel, to sentire *sayn-teeray*
fennel finocchio *fee-nok-kyo*
few/a qualche *kwal-kay*
fig fico *fee-ko*
filled ripieno *ree-pee-ayno*
fillet filetto *feelayt-to*
filter, to filtrare *feel-trahray*
find, to trovare *tro-vahray*
fine sottile *so-teel-lay*
finish, to finire *fee-neeray*
fire fuoco *fwoko*
first prima *preema*
fish pesce *payshay*
fish soup brodetto (di pesce) *bro-det-to (dee payshay)*
fishing pesca *payska*
fizzy frizzante *freedz-zantay*; gassato/a *gas-sato*
flakes fiocchi *fee-yok-kee*
flame fiamma *fee-yahm-ma*

flat piatto *pee-at-to*
flavor gusto *goosto*; sapore *sa-pohray*
flavor, to insaporire *eensa-po-ree-ay*
flavoring condimento *kondee-maynto*
flight volo *vohloh*
floor piano *pee-ah-no*
Florence Firenze *fee-rentsay*
flour farina *fa-reena*
flower fiore *feeo-ray*
fly mosca *moska*
food dyes coloranti *ko-loh-ran-tee*
food poisoning intossicazione alimentare *eentos-seekats-yohnay alee-mayn-tahray*
foot piede *pee-e-day*
for per *payr*
foreign straniero(a) *stran-yero/a*
foreigner straniero(a) *stran-yero/a*
forget, to dimenticare *dee-mayn-tee-kahray*
fork forchetta *forkayt-ta*
forward avanti *avan-tee*
France Francia *fran-cha*
frankfurter würstel *voor-stel*
free gratuito(a) *grat-too-eeto/a*; libero(a) *lee-bay-ro/a*
French francese *fran-chayzay*
fresh fresco(a) *fraysko/a*
fresh fruit frutta fresca *froot-ta frayska*
fresh mushrooms funghi freschi *foongee frayskee*;
Friday venerdì *vaynayr-dee*
fried fritto(a) *freet-to*
fried pastry twist crespelle *kray-spel-lay*
friend amico(a) *a-meeko/a*

fritters frittelle *freet-tel-lay*
frozen congelato(a) *konjay-lahto*; surgelato(a) *soorjay-lahto*
fruit frutta *froot-ta*
fruit salad macedonia *machay-don-ya*
fruits of the forest frutti di bosco *froot-tee dee bosko*
frying pan padella *padel-la*; tegame *tay-gamay*
full pieno(a) *pee-e-no/a*
full-bodied corposo(a) *kohr-po-zo/a*; robusto *ro-boosto*

game (animal) cacciagione *kat-cha-jonay*
game (hunting) selvaggina *sayl-vad-jeena*
garden giardino *jar-deeno*
garlic aglio *al-yo*
garnishing guarnizione *gwar-niz-eeonay*
gender genere *je-nayray*
Genoa Genova *je-nova*
gentleman signore *seen-yohray*
genuine autentico *owten-teeko*
German tedesco(a) *tay-daysko/a*
Germany Germania *jer-ma-nee-a*
get, to ottenere *ot-taynayr-ray*
gherkin cetriolini *chaytree-o-lee-nee*
ginger zenzero *dzen-dzayro*
girl ragazza *ragats-sa*
give, to dare *dahray*
glass bicchiere *beek-ye-ray*; vetro *vaytro*
glasses occhiali *ok-kyahlee*
gloves guanti *gwantee*
go, to andare *an-dahray*
gold oro *ohro*
golden brown dorato(a) *do-rato*
good bene *benay*; buono(a)

goose oca *oka*
go out/come out, to uscire *oo-sheeray*
grain filo *feel-lo*; grano *grano*
grapefruit pompelmo *pom-pelmo*
grapes uva *oova*
grated grattugiato(a) *grat-too-jato*
gray mullet cefalo *che-fa-lo*
greasy unto(a) *oon-to/a*
great grande *granday*
Great Britain Gran Bretagna *gran braytan-ya*
Greece Grecia *gret-cha*
Greek greco(a) *gre-ko*
green verde *vayrday*
grill griglia *greel-ya*
grilled steak bistecca ai ferri *bee-stayk-ka i ferry*
group comitiva *koh-meeteeva*; gruppo *groop-po*
group-leader capogruppo *kapo-groop-po*
grouper cernia *cher-nee-a*
guard, to custodire *koo-sto-deeray*
guide guida *gweeda*
guide book guida *gweeda*
guinea fowl faraona *fa-ra-ohna*

hake nasello *na-zello*
half metà *mayta*
hall sala *sala*
ham prosciutto *proshoot-to*
hand mano *mahno*
handbag borsetta *bors-aytta*
handkerchief fazzoletto di carta *fats-so-layt-to dee karta*
happen, to succedere *soot-che-dayray*
happy contento(a) *kon-tento*

hard duro(a) *dooro/a*; sodo *sohdo*
hare lepre *lepray*
harmless innocuo(a) *een-nok-wo*
harsh duro(a) *dooro/a*
hat cappello *kap-pel-lo*
have, to avere *a-vayray*
have to, to dovere *do-vayray*
hazlenuts nocciole *not-cholay*
headache mal di testa *mal dee testa*
hear, to sentire *sayn-teeray*
heat, to riscaldare *reeskal-dahray*
heating riscaldamento *reeskal-da-maynto*
heavy pesante *pay-zan-tay*
help, to aiutare *a-yoo-tahray*
helping porzione *por-zeeonay*
hen gallina *gal-leena*
herbs erbe aromatiche *erbay aro-mahtee-kay*
here qui *kwee*
herring aringa *a-rin-ga*
high chair seggiolone *sayd-jo-lohnay*
high-proof spirits superalcolici *soopayr-alkol-leechee*
hire noleggio *nolayd-jo*
hold, to tenere *tay-nayray*
holiday festa *fe-sta*
holidays ferie *fe-ree-ay*; vacanza *va-kantsa*
Holland Olanda *o-landa*
honey miele *mee-elay*
honey mushrooms chiodini *kee-odee-nee*
hors-d'oeuvre antipasto *an-tee-pasto*
hospital ospedale *ospay-dahlay*
hot caldo(a) *kaldo/a*
hotel albergo *al-bayr-go*
hour ora *ohra*
how come *kohmay*

how much/many quanto *kwanto* quanti *kwantee*
hundred cento *chen-to*
hunger fame *fahmay*
hurry fretta *frayt-ta*
husband marito *ma-reeto*

ice ghiaccio *geeat-cho*
ice-cream gelato *jay-lahto*
ice-cream shop gelateria *jay-lah-tay-reea*
ice-cube cubetto di ghiaccio *koo-bayt-to dee geeat-cho*
ice lolly ghiacciolo *geeat-cholo*
icing glassa *glas-sa*
identity card carta di identità *karta dee ee-den-tee-ta*
ill malato(a) *ma-lahto/a*
immediately subito *soo-beeto*
important importante *eempor-tan-tay*
impossible impossibile *eempos-see-beelay*
in dentro *dayntro*
in cash in contanti *een kon-tan-tee*
in front davanti *da-vantee*
in order that perché *payrkay*
in order to per *payr*
included compreso *kom-prayzo*
inclusive incluso(a) *een-kloo-zo*
indoors al coperto *al ko-payrto*
inexpensive economico(a) *ayko-no-meeko/a*
inform, to avvertire *av-vayr-teeray*; informare *een-for-mahray*
information informazioni *een-for-mats-yohnee*
infusion tisana *tee-zan-na*
inn osteria *os-tayr-eea*
insect insetto *een-set-to*
inside dentro *dayntro*; interno

een-*tay*rno
instead invece *een-vay*chay
invite, to invitare *een-vee-tah*ray
invoice fattura *fat-too*ra
Ireland Irlanda *eer-lan*da
Italian italiano(a) *eetal-yah*no
Italy Italia *eetal-*ya

jacket giacca *jak*-ka
jam confettura *kon-fayt-too*ra;
  marmellata *mahrmayl-lah*ta
jam tart crostata *kros-ta*-ta
January gennaio *jen-na*-yo
jelly gelatina *jayla-tee*na
job posto *pos*to
jug brocca *brok*-ka
juice succo *sook*-ko
July luglio *lool*-yo
June giugno *joon*-yo
juniper ginepro *jin-ep*ro
just solo *solo*

keep, to tenere *tay-nay*ray
keeper custode *koo-sto*day
khaki cachi *ka*-kee
kid (gloves) capretto *kap-prayt*to
kidney (food) rognone *ron-yoh-*nay
kind (type) genere *jay*nayray
kitchen cucina *koo-chee*na
kiwi kiwi *kee-wee*
knife coltello *koltel*-lo
know, to sapere *sa-pay*ray

label etichetta *ay-tee-kayt*ta
lady signora *seen-yoh*ra
lager birra chiara *beer*-ra *kee-ara*
lake lago *lah*go
lamb abbacchio *ab-bakee-*o;
  agnello *an-yel*-lo; castrato
  kastrat-to

land paese *pa-ay*zay
lard lardo *lardo*
large grande *gran*day
last ultimo(a) *ool-teemo/a*
laugh riso *ree*zo
laurel alloro *al-lor*-o
lean magro(a) *magro/a*
leave, to lasciare *lashah*ray; partire *par-tee*ray
leeks porri *por*-ree
leg gamba *gamba*
lemon limone *lee-moh*nay
lemonade limonata *leemo-nah*ta
lentils lenticchie *len-teek-kee*ay
less meno *may*-no
let, to lasciare *lashah*ray
let go of, to lasciare *lashah*ray
lettuce lattuga *lat-too*ga
lift ascensore *ashayn-soh*ray
light leggero *lay-jay*-ro luce *loo*chay
light, to accendere *at-chen-day*ray
like come *koh*may
like, to gradire *gra-dee*ray
line linea *lee*nay-a
liqueur liquore *lee-kwoh*ray
liqueur glass bicchierino *beek-ye-ree*no
list elenco *ay-len*ko; lista *lee*sta
lit acceso(a) *at-chay*-zo
liter litro *lee*tro
little piccolo(a) *peek-*kolo/a;
  poco(a) *po*-ko/a
liver fegato *fay-*gato
lobster aragosta *ara-go*sta; astice *astee-*chay
loin lombata *lom-ba*ta
long lungo(a) *loon*go/a
lose, to perdere *payr*dayray
loud forte *for*-tay

lovely bello(a) _bel-lo_
lunch colazione _kola-tsyohnay_;
pranzo _prantso_

mackerel sgombro _sgom-bro_
macrobiotic macrobiotico
macro-bee-ot-teeko
maize granturco _gran-toorko_; mais
ma-ees
make, to fare _fahray_
management direzione _deerayts-
yonay_
mandarin mandarino _mandar-
reeno_
manner modo _moh-do_
map pianta _peeantha_
March marzo _martso_
marinate marinata _ma-ree-nahta_
market mercato _mayr-kahto_
marmalade confettura _kon-fay-
toora_; marmellata _mahrmayl-laht-
ta_
marrow zucca _dzook-ka_
match fiammifero _fee-am-mee-
fayro_
mature maturo(a) _ma-tooro/a_; sta-
gionato(a) _sta-joh-nahto_
May maggio _mad-jo_
mayonnaise maionese _ma-yo-
nayzay_
meal pasto _pasto_
meaning significato _seeg-neefee-
kahto_
means mezzo _medz-zo_
meat carne _karnay_;
meatballs polpette _pol-payttay_
medicine medicina _maydee-chee-
na_
meet, to incontrare _eenkon-trahray_
melon melone _may-lohnay_
menu menu _may-noo_
meringue meringa _may-reenga_

message comunicazione _koh-
moon-ee-kats-yoh-nay_
middle mezzo _medz-zo_
Milan Milano _mee-lahno_
milk latte _laht-tay_
mince, to tritare _tree-tahray_;
minced tritato _tree-tahto_
mineral water acqua minerale
akwa meenay-rahlay
mint menta _maynta_
minus meno _may-no_
minute minuto _mee-nooto_
Miss (young woman) signorina
seen-yoh-reena
mistake errore _ayr-rohray_
misunderstanding malinteso _mal-
leen-tayzo_
mix misto(a) _mee-sto/a_
mixed misto(a) _mee-sto/a_
molluscs molluschi _moh-looskee_
Monday lunedì _loonay-dee_
month mese _mayzay_
monuments monumenti _monoo-
mayntee_
more più _pee-oo_
morning mattina _mat-teena_
mosquitoes zanzare _dzan-
dzahray_
most più _pee-oo_
mother madre _mahdray_
mouth bocca _bok-ka_
much molto _mohlto_
mullet triglie _treelyay_
museum museo _moozay-o_
mushrooms funghi _foongee_;
music musica _moo-zeeka_
mussels cozze _kots-say_
must dovere _do-vayray_
mustard senape _se-napay_
mutton castrato _kastrat-to_

name nome _nohmay_

napkin/serviette tovagliolo *toval-yolo*
Naples Napoli *nah-polee*
narrow stretto(a) *stray-to/a*
nearby accanto *ak-kanto*
nearly quasi *kwahzee*
need bisogno *beezon-yo;*
never mai *ma-ee*
newspaper giornale *jor-nahlay*
New Year's Day Capodanno *kapo-danno*
no nessuno(a) *nays-soono/a*
nobody nessuno(a) *nays-soono/a*
noise rumore *roomohray*
noisy rumoroso(a) *roomo-rohzo/a*
non-alcoholic analcolico *anal-koleeko*
non-smoker non-fumatore *nohn fooma-tohray*
none nessuno(a) *nays-soono*
noodles pastina *pas-teena*
north nord *nord*
not much poco(a) *po-ko/a*
nothing niente *nee-entay*
nourishment alimentazione *alee-mayn-tahts-yo-nay*
November novembre *novem-bray*
now ora *ohra*
number numero *noo-mayro*
nutcracker schiaccianoci *skee-atcha-nochee*
nutmeg noce moscata *no-chay mos-kata*

oats avena *avay-na*
obligatory obbligatorio *ob-blee-ga-tor-yo*
obtain, to ottenere *ot-tenay-ray*
October ottobre *ot-tohbray*
odor odore *o-dohray*
offal frattaglie *fra-tal-yay*
often spesso *spays-so*

oil olio *ol-yo*
oily unto(a) *oon-to/a*
old vecchio(a) *vayk-yo/a*
olives olive *o-leevay*
omelette frittata *free-tat-ta*
on avanti *avan-tee;* sopra *sohpra*
on foot a piedi *a pee-e-dee*
on top sopra *sohpra*
onion cipolla *cheepohl-la*
only solamente *sola-mayntay;* solo *solo*
open/open air aperto *a-payr-to/-* all'aperto *al-a-payr-to*
opposite davanti *da-vantee*
orange arancia *a-rancha*
orangesoda aranciata *a-ran-cha-ta*
order ordinazione *ordee-nats-yohnay*
order, to ordinare *ordee-nahray*
oregano origano *oree-gano*
original autentico *owten-teeko*
other altro *altro*
out of order guasto *gwasto*
outfit insieme *een-see-emay*
outside esterno(a) *ay-ster-no/a;* fuori *fworee*
oven forno *forno*
over sopra *sohpra*
overseas straniero(a) *stran-yero/a*
own proprio *prop-reeo*
ox bue *boo-ay*
oysters ostriche *os-treekay*

packet busta *boo-sta*
pain male *mahlay*
pair paio *pa-yo*
pale chiaro(a) *keea-ro*
parents genitori *jaynee-tohree*
park parco *parko*
Parmesan parmigiano *par-mee-jano*

parsley prezzemolo *prayts-say-molo*

part parte *partay*

party comitiva *koh-mee-teeva*; festa *fay-sta*

passport passaporto *pas-sa-porto*

pasta pasta *pasta*

pastry pasta *pasta*

pay, to pagare *pa-gahray*

payment pagamento *paga-maynto*

peach pesca *peska*

peanut arachide *arakeeday*

pear pera *payra*

peas piselli *peezel-lee*

peep, to sbucciare *sboot-chahray*

pencil matita *ma-tee-ta*

pepper pepe *paypay*

pepper (vegetable) peperone *paypay-ronay*

pepper-mill macinapepe *ma-cheena-paypay*

per per *payr*

perch pesce persico *payshay per-seeko*

perhaps forse *for-say*

permission permesso *payr-mays-so*

permit permesso *payr-mays-so*

pharmacy farmacia *farma-chee-a*

pheasant fagiano *fa-jano*

photograph fotografia *foto-gra-fee-a*

pickles sottaceti *sot-achay-tee*

pie torta *tor-ta*

piece pezzo *pets-so*

pig maiale *ma-yahlay*

pigeon piccione *peet-chonay*

pill pillola *peel-lola*

pillow cuscino *koo-sheeno*

pineapple ananas *a-nanas*

pistachio nuts pistacchi *pees-takkee*

place/cover charge coperto *ko-payrto;*

place locale *loh-calay*; luogo *lwoh-go*

plan piano *pee-ah-no*

plaster/Band Aid (USA) cerotto *chayrot-to*

plate piatto *pee-at-to*

play, to giocare *jo-kahray*; suonare *soo-ohnahray*

please per favore *payr fa-vohray*

pleasure piacere *pee-a-chayray*

plums prugne *proon-yay*

plus più *pee-oo*

point out, to avvertire *av-vayr-teeray*

pork maiale *ma-yahlay*

pork meats suino *soo-eeno*

portion porzione *por-zeeonay*

position posto *posto*

possible possibile *pos-see-beelay*

postcard cartolina *karto-leena*

pot pentola *payn-tola*

potatoes patate *pa-tahtay*

pounded (meat) macinato *ma-cheena-to;*

power (electricity) corrente *kohr-rentay*

pram carrozzina *kar-rots-seena*

prawns gamberi *gam-bayree*

prefer, to preferire *prayfay-reeray*

pregnant incinta *een-cheenta*

prepare, to preparare *praypa-rahray*

prescription ricetta *reechet-ta*

preservatives conservanti *kon-sayr-vantee*

preserved conservato(a) *kon-sayr-vato/a*

price prezzo *prets-so*

pudding budino *boo-dee-no*

puff pastry pasta sfoglia *pastasfol-ya*

pulp polpa *pol-pa*

pumpkin zucca *dzoo-ka*

purpose fine *feenay*

put mettere _mayt_-tayray

quail quaglia _kwal_-ya
quarter quarto(a) _kwarto/a_
question domanda _do-manda_
quick veloce _vay-lohchay_
quickly velocemente _vaylo-chay-mayntay_
quietly piano _pee-ah-no_

rabbit coniglio _koneel-yo_
radio radio _rahd-yo_
radishes ravanelli _rava-nayl-lee_
raincoat impermeabile _eempayr-may-ah-beelay_
raisins uvetta _oovayt-ta_
raspberries lamponi _lam-pohnee_
raw crudo(a) _kroodo_
read, to leggere _lej-jeray_
ready pronto(a) _pronto/a_
ready-made confezionato(a) _kon-fayts-yonato/a_
really proprio _prop-reeo_
receipt ricevuta _reechay-voota_
recipe ricetta _reechet-ta_
red rosso(a) _ros-so(a)_
refrigerator frigorifero _freego-ree-fayro_
refund rimborso _reem-borso_
region regione _ray-jonay_
remain, to restare _ray-stahray_; rimanere _ree-man-ayray_
remainder resto _resto_
remove, to togliere _tol-yayray_
reply, to rispondere _ree-spondayray_
reservation prenotazione _prayno-tats-yonay_
reserve, to prenotare _prayno-tah-ray_; riservare _ree-sayr-vahray_
reserved riservato(a) _ree-sayrva-to/a_

resort stazione _stats-yohnay_
respond, to rispondere _ree-spon-dayray_
restaurant ristorante _reesto-rantay_
return ritorno _ree-torno_; ritornare _ree-tor-nahray_
ribs costine _kos-teenay_
rice riso _reezo_
right (legal) diritto _deereet-to_; destra _destra_ **on the right** a destra a _destra_
ripe maturo/a _ma-tooro/a_
rise, to salire _sa-leeray_
road strada _strahda_
roast arrosto _ar-rosto_
roasted arrostito _ar-rostee-to_
roll panino _pa-neeno_
Rome Roma _rohma_
room camera _ka-mayra_: locale _loh-kahlay_; stanza _stantsa_
room temperature temperatura ambiente _taympay-ra-toora am-byentay_
rosé rosato _ro-zato_;
rosemary rosmarino _rohz-maree-no_
round intorno _een-tor-no_
rump fesa _fay-za_
runner beans fagiolini _fa-joleenee_
rural rustico(a) _roo-steeko_

safety pin spilla di sicurezza _speel-la dee seekoo-rayts-sa_
saffron zafferano _dzaf-fayr-rahno_
sage salvia _sal-veea_
salad insalata _eensa-lahta_
salmon salmone _sal-mohnay_
salt sale _sahlay_
salt shaker saliera _salee-ayra_
salted salato(a) _sa-laht-to/a_
salty salato(a) _sa-laht-to/a_
same stesso(a) _stays-so/a_; uguale

oo-gwal-lay
sandwich tramezzino _tra-medz-zeeno_
sardines sardine _sar-deenay_
Sardinia Sardegna _sardayn-ya_
Saturday sabato _sa-bato_
sauce intingolo _een-teeng-golo;_ salsa _salsa_; sugo _soogo_
sausages insaccati _een-sak-katee_; salsiccia _salseet-cha_
savory salato(a) _sal-lah-to_
say dire _deeray_
scampi scampi _skampee_
schedule orario _ohr-rar-eeo_
scour, to sgrassare _sgras-sahray_
scrambled eggs uova strapazzate _wova strapats-sahtay_
sea mare _mahray_
sea-bream pagello _pa-jello_
seafood frutti di mare _froot-tee dee mahray_
seaside mare _mahray_
season stagione _sta-jonay_
season, to insaporire _eensa-po-reeray_
seasoning condimento _kondee-maynto_
seat posto _posto_
second secondo(a) _say-kohndo/a_
sedative calmante _kal-mantay_
see, to vedere _vay-dayray_
sell, to vendere _vayn-dayray_
semolina semolino _saymo-leeno_
September settembre _sayt-tembray_
service (charge) servizio _sayrveets-yo_
set the table, to apparecchiare _ap-pa-rayk-keea-ray_
settle, to (wine) depositare _daypo-zee-taray_
shake frappé _frap-pay_
share parte _partay_
shell conchiglia _kohn-keel-ya;_

guscio _goo-sho_
shellfish crostacei _kros-ta-chay-ee_
shop negozio _naygots-yo_
shopping trolley/ shopping cart (USA) carrello _kar-rel-lo_
short crust pastry pasta frolla _pasta frol-la_
shoulder spalla _spal-la_
show (performance) spettacolo _spayt-tah-kolo_
show, to mostrare _mo-strahray_
shrimps gamberi _gam-bayree_
Sicily Sicilia _seecheel-ya_
sick malato(a) _ma-lahto/a_
side parte _partay_
signature firma _feerma_
simple semplice _saym-pleechay_
skewers spiedini _speeay-deenee_
slice fetta _fayt-ta_
sliced affettato _a-fayt-tahto_
slip, to sgusciare _sgoo-shahray_
slowly piano _pee-ahno_
small piccolo(a) _peek-kolo/a_
smell odore _o-dohray_
smoke, to fumare _foo-mahray_
smoked affumicato _af-foomee-kahto_
smoked bacon pancetta affumicata _panchayt-ta af-foomee-kahta_
smoked salmon salmone affumicato _sal-mohnay af-foomee-kahto_
smoker fumatore _foo-mah-toray_
smooth liscio(a) _lee-sho/a_
snack merenda _may-renda;_ spuntino _spoon-teeno_
snack bar tavola calda _tah-vola kalda_
snails lumache _loo-ma-kay_
soap sapone _sa-pohnay_
sole sogliola _sol-yohla_
some alcuni _al-koonee;_ qualche _kwal-kay_

somebody qualcuno kwal-_koo_no
something qualcosa kwal-_ko_za
son figlio _feel_-yo
song canzone kant-_soh_nay
sorbet sorbetto sor-_bayt_-to
soup minestra mee-_nes_tra; brodo broh-do; zuppa _dzoop_-pa
sour acerbo a-_cher_-bo; acido _a_-chee-do; agro _ag_ro
sour cherry tree amarena a-mah-_ray_-na
south sud sood
soya soia _so_-ya
sparkling frizzante freedz-_zantay_
sparkling water acqua gassata _akwa_ gas-_sa_-ta
spiced aromatico a-ro-_mat_tee-ko
spices spezie _spay_-zeeay
spicy piccante peek-_kan_tay
spinach spinaci spee-_na_chee
spit spiedo spee-_ay_do
spoon cucchiaio kook-_ya_-yo;
square piazza pee-_at_ssa ; carré kar-_ray_
squid calamari kala-_ma_ree
squill canocchia ka-_nok_-ya
stairs scale _ska_hlay
stamp francobollo franko-_bohl_-lo
starch amido _a_-meedo
start inizio een-_eets_-yo
start, to cominciare komeen-_chah_-ray
station stazione stats-_yoh_nay
stay, to restare ray-_stah_ray
steak bistecca bee_stayk_-ka;
steam vapore va-_poh_ray
steamed vapore va-_poh_ray
stew spezzatino spets-sa_tee_-no; stufato stoo-_fah_to
stewed lessato(a) lays-_sah_-to
still ancora an-_ko_ra
still water acqua naturale _akwa_

na-toor-_ah_-lay
stomach-ache mal di stomaco mal dee _sto_-ma-ko
stop (bus) fermata fayr-_mah_-ta
stop, to fermare fayr-_mah_ray
stopper tappo _tap_-po
stout birra scura _beer_-ra skoora
straight liscio(a) _lee_-sho/a
straight on diritto dee_reet_-to
strait (sea) stretto(a) _strayt_-to/a
strawberry fragola _frah_gola
street strada _strah_da; via _vee_-a
stuffed farcito(a) fahr-_chee_to
stuffing ripieno ree-pee-_ay_no
subtle sottile sot-_teel_-lay
such as come _koh_may
sugar zucchero _tsook_-kayro
sugar-bowl zuccheriera tsook-kayree-_ay_ra
sugar-coated almonds confetti kon-_fet_-tee
suitcase valigia va-_lee_ja
summer estate ay-_stah_tay
summery estivo(a) ay-_stee_voh
Sunday domenica _do_may-neeka
supper cena _chay_na
surname cognome kon-_yoh_may
surroundings dintorni deen-_tohr_-nee
sweet caramella kara-_mel_la; dolce _dol_chay
sweet bread animelle anee-_me_-lay
sweetener dolcificante dohl-chee-fee-_kan_tay
sweets dolciumi dohl-_choo_-mee
swim, to nuotare nwo-_tah_ray
swimming pool piscina pee-_shee_na
Switzerland Svizzera _zveet_-sayra
swordfish pesce spada _pay_shay spada

syrup sciroppo *shee-rop-po*

table tavola/tavolo *tah-vola/o*
table-cloth tovaglia *toval-ya*
tablet pastiglia *pasteel-ya*
tag etichetta *ay-tee-kaytta*
take, to prendere *pren-dayray*
take away, to togliere *tol-yayray*
talcum powder borotalco *boro-talko*
tap rubinetto *rube-nay-toh*
tart torta *tor-ta*
taste assaggio *as-sad-jo*; gusto *goosto*
taste, to assaggiare *as-sad-jahray*; gustare *goo-stahray*
tea tè *tay*
teaspoon cucchiaino *kook-kya-eeno*
telephone telefono *tayle-fono*; **on the telephone** al telefono *al tayle-fono*
telephone call chiamata *keea-mahta*; telefonata *taylayfo-nahta*
telephone directory elenco telefonico *ay-lenko taylay-fo-neeko*
temperature temperatura *taym-pay-ra-toora*
tender tenero(a) *te-nayro/a*
terminal (station) capolinea *kapo-leenay-a*
terrace terrazza *tayr-rats-sa*
thank ringraziare *reen-grats-yahray*
thank you grazie *grats-yay*
that (prep.) che *kay*
that quello(a) *kwayl-lo*
then poi *poy*
thick grosso/a *gros-so/a*
thin magro(a) *magro/a*
thing cosa *kosa*
thirst sete *saytay*

this questo(a) *kwaysto/a*
thousand mille *meel-lay*
thread filo *fee-lo*
throat gola *gohla*
throw, to gettare *jayt-tahray*
Thursday giovedì *jovay-dee*
thyme timo *tee-mo*
ticket biglietto *beel-yayt-to*
tie cravatta *kravat-ta*
tight stretto(a) *strayt-to/a*
timbale sformato(a) *sfor-mahto/a*
time tempo *tempo*
timetable orario *oh-rar-eeo*
tin-opener apriscatole *apree-skah-tolay*
tinned meat carne in scatola *karnay een ska-to-la*
tip mancia *mancha*
titbits bocconcini *bok-on-cheenee*
toast, to brindare *breen-dah-ray*
toasted abbrustolito *ab-broo-sto-leeto*; arrostito *ar-rostee-to*; tostato(a) *to-stahto/a*
tobacconist's shop tabaccheria *tabak-kayrreea*
today oggi *od-jee*
together insieme *een-see-emay*
toilet toilette *twalet*
tomato pomodoro *pomo-doro*
tomorrow domani *do-mahnee*
tongue lingua *leengwa*
tonight stasera *sta-sayra*
too anche *ankay*
too much troppo *trop-po*
toothpick stecchino *stay-keeno*; stuzzicadenti *stoots-seeka-dentee*
total totale *totah-le*
tough duro(a) *dooro/a*
tour giro *jeero*
toward(s) verso *vayrso*
towel asciugamano *ashoo-ga-mahno*

train treno *trayn-no*
transport trasporto *tra-spor-to*
tray vassoio *vas-so-yo*
tripe trippa *treep-pa*
trout trota *trot-ta*
truffle tartufo *tahr-toofo*
try, to provare *pro-vahray*
Tuesday martedì *martay-dee*
tunafish tonno *ton-no*
turbot rombo *rombo*
tureen terrina *tayr-reena*
Turin Torino *to-reeno*
turkey tacchino *tak-keeno*
turn giro *jeero*
turn, to girare *jee-rahray*
turn off, to spegnere *spayn-yayray*
turn on, to accendere *at-chen-dayray*
turned on acceso(a) *at-chay-zo*
turnips rape *rahpay*

ugly brutto(a) *broot-to/a*
umbrella ombrello *ombrel-lo*
uncomfortable scomodo(a) *sko-modo(a)*
uncooked crudo(a) *kroodo*
uncork (uncap), to stappare *stap-pahray*
under sotto *soht-to*
underneath sotto *soht-to*
understand, to capire *ka-peeray*
United States of America Stati Uniti (d'America) *stahtee oo-neetee damayr-reeka*
until fino a *feeno a*
upbringing allevamento *al-lay-vah-mayn-to*
use, to usare *oo-zahray*

V.A.T. I.V.A. *eeva*
vacant libero(a) *lee-bay-ro/a*
vanilla vaniglia *va-neelya*

veal vitello *veetayl-lo*
vegetables contorno *kohn-tor-noh;* /legumi *lay-goo-mee;* ortaggi *or-tadjee;* verdure *vayr-dooray*
vegetables (raw) crudità *kroo-dee-ta*
vegetarian vegetariano(a) *vayjay-tar-yahno*
Venice Venezia *vaynayts-ya*
very molto *mohlto*
vinegar aceto *a-chayto*
vitamins vitamine *veeta-meenay*

wait, to aspettare *aspayt-tahray;* attendere *at-ten-dayray*
waiter cameriere *kamayr-ye-ray*
waitress cameriera *kamayr-ye-ra*
walk, to camminare *ka-mee-naray*
wall muro *moo-ro*
wallet portafoglio *porta-fol-yo*
walnuts/nuts noci *nochee*
want, to volere *vo-layray*
wardrobe guardaroba *gwarda-roba*
warm, to scaldare *skal-daray*
warn, to avvertire *av-ver-teeray*
wash, to lavare *la-vahray*
wasp vespa *vespa*
watch orologio *oro-lojo*
watch (look at), to guardare *gwar-dahray*
water acqua *akwa*
watermelon anguria *an-goo-reea;* cocomero *ko-komay-ro*
waterproof impermeabile *eem-payr-may-ah-beelay*
way modo *moh-do*
weak debole *day-bolay*
wear, to portare *por-tahray*
Wednesday mercoledì *mayrko-laydee*
week settimana *sayt-tee-mahna*

weekday feriale *fayr-yahlay*
welcome benvenuto *baynvay-nooto*
well bene *benay*
wet (paint) fresco(a) *fraysko/a*
what does it mean? cosa significa? *koza seeg-neefeeka*
what happened? cosa è successo? *koza e soot-ches-so*
what che *kay*
when quando *kwando*
where dove *dovay*
whereas mentre *mayntray*
which che *kay*; chi *kee*; quale *kwale*
while mentre *mayntray*
white bianco *bee-anko*
who che *kay*; chi *kee*
whole intero(a) *een-tayro*
wholemeal integrale *een-tay-gra-lay*
why come *kohmay*; perché *payrkay*
wife moglie *mol-yay*
window finestra *fee-nestra*

wine vino *veeno*
wine shop cantina *kan-tee-na*
winter inverno *een-vayrno*
wire filo *feel-lo*
with con *kohn*
without senza *sentsa*
without tomatoes (usually refers to pasta or pizza) in bianco *een bee-anko*
woman donna *don-na*
word parola *pa-rola*
work lavoro *lavoro*
work (mechanism) funzionare *foon-zeeo-nahray*
write, to scrivere *skree-vayray*

year (ref. to wine) annata *an-nah-ta*; anno *an-no*
yeast lievito *lee-ay-veeto*
yellow giallo(a) *jal-lo*
yesterday ieri *yeree*
yet ancora *an-kora*
yoghurt yogurt *yogurt*
yolk tuorlo *twohr-lo*
young giovane *joh-vanay*

INDEX

In the same series:

How to Eat Out in Italy
How to Eat Out in France
How to Eat Out in Spain
How to Eat Out in Russia
How to Eat Out in Greece
How to Eat Out in Portugal & Brazil